# KRONOS, SHIVA, & ASKLEPIOS

## Studies in Magical Gems and Religions
## of the Roman Empire

# KRONOS, SHIVA, & ASKLEPIOS

## Studies in Magical Gems and Religions
## of the Roman Empire

Attilio Mastrocinque

American Philosophical Society
Philadelphia • 2011

Transactions of the
American Philosophical Society
Held at Philadelphia
For Promoting Useful Knowledge
Volume 101, Part 5

ISBN: 978-1-60618-015-0

US ISSN: 0065-9746


Library of Congress Cataloguing-in-Publication Data

Mastrocinque, Attilio.
  Kronos, Shiva, and Asklepios : studies in magical gems and religions of the Roman
Empire / Attilio Mastrocinque.
     p. cm. — (Transactions of the American Philosophical Society ; v. 101, pt. 5)
  Includes bibliographical references and index.
  ISBN 978-1-60618-015-0
  1. Gems—Rome—Miscellanea. 2. Magic—Rome. 3. Rome—Religion. 4. Cronus (Greek
deity) 5. Siva (Hindu deity) 6. Asklepios (Greek deity) I. Title.
  BF1442.P74M37 2012
  133.4'4—dc23
                          2012007684

# Contents

# Preface

This volume presents a series of analyses of peculiar iconographies and texts concerning magical gems. Magical gems are amulets created by carving words or symbols into precious stones; most were made during the Roman Empire. Magical gems are compounds created by modern scholars in which a variety of beliefs can be recognized. These documents provide us with many interesting approaches, from the point of view of magical medicine, of linguistic features of magical words, of the merging of Graeco-Roman and Eastern iconographies, and so on. My purpose here is to use the iconographies and the texts about magical gems as documents to understand the most refined religious thought of Imperial Age theologists. During the Imperial Age, gems were often seen as tools used to cope with the problems of common daily life; for modern scholars they preserve elements of ancient theological and cosmological theories. Even the most banal problems were faced by appealing to the higher gods and using sophisticated divine names and iconographies. In several cases we know of these names and images only through magical gems.

This small book gathers five studies on magical gems and religions of the Roman Empire. The first, second, and fifth chapters deal with topics that I have previously explored;[1] but this volume presents texts and archaeological evidence in a new way. The research on Shiva–Helios and Asklepios of Ascalon are the result of my studies of the magical gems in Italy and of those in the Cabinet des Médailles in France. I realize that this topic is very obscure and I will try to explain myself avoiding rare or unusual words. The varying degrees of reliability of my proposals will be clarified by my putting hypotheses in the footnotes and more plausible explanations in the text. I hope to offer some new perspectives on the intriguing, elusive, and intricate religious environments that existed during the Imperial Age in Egypt and the Near East.

I thank very much all the scholars who helped during my research and improved the results, in particular Pierre Amandry, Mathilde Avisseau Broustet, Silvana Balbi De Caro, Glen Bowersock, Christopher Faraone, Teresa Giove, Patricia A. Johnston, Kennet Lapatin, Simone Michel, Elizabeth Ann Pollard, and Erika Zwierlein-Diehl.

# Abbreviations

AE: *Année Épigraphique*
AGDS: *Antike Gemmen in deutschen Sammlungen*
AIPhO: *Annuaire de l'Institut de Philologie et d'Histoire Orientales*
AJA: *American Journal of Archaeology*
AMNS: *American Numismatic Society*
ANSMN: *American Numismatic Society. Museum Notes*
ARW: *Archiv für Religionswissenschaft*
ASAE: *Annales du Service des antiquités de l'Égypte*
BCAR: *Bollettino della Commissione Archeologica Comunale di Roma*
BMC: *British Museum Catalogue*
Bonner, SMA: C. Bonner, *Studies in Magical Amulets chiefly
    Graeco-Egyptian*
Chr. d'Eg.: *Chronique d'Égypte*
CIL: *Corpus Inscriptionum Latinarum* (Berlin: 1862).
CIMRM: M.J. Vermaseren, *Corpus inscriptionum et monumentorum
    religionis Mithriacae*, I–II, (den Haag: 1954, 1960).
CPh: *The Classical Philology*
Delatte, Derchain: A. Delatte and Ph. Derchain, *Les intailles magiques
    gréco-égyptiennes*
EPRO: *Études préliminaires aux religions orientales dans l'empire romain*
    (Leiden: 1961).
GCS: *Die griechischen christlichen Schriftsteller der ersten drei Jahrhund-
    erte* (Berlin: 1897, 2008).
GGA: Göttingische Gelehrte Anzeigen
GMPT: *The Greek Magical Papyri in Translation*, H.D. Betz, ed.
IDélos: *Inscriptions de Délos* (Paris: 1926, 2008).
IEJ: *Israel Explorations Journal*

IGLS: *Les inscriptions grecques et latines de la Syrie* (Paris: 1929, 2009).

JANER: *Journal of Ancient Near Eastern Religions*

JbAC: *Jahrbuch für Antike und Christentum*

JNES: *Journal of Near Eastern Studies*

JWCI: *Journal of the Warburg and Courtauld Institutes*

LIMC: *Lexicon Iconographicum Mythologiae Classicae* (Zürich: 1981–2009).

MDAI(K): *Mitteilungen des deutschen archäologischen Institutes (Kairoer Abteilung)*

MEFRA: *Mélanges de l'École Française de Rome (Antiquité)*

Michel, *British Museum*: S. Michel, *Die magischen Gemmen im Britischen Museum*

MUB: *Mélanges de la Faculté Orientale de l'Université Saint Joseph. Beyrouth*

NHC: Nag Hammadi Codices

PawB: Potsdamer Altertumswissenschaftliche Beiträge

PGM: *Papyri Graecae Magicae. Die griechischen Zauberpapyri*

PO: *Patrologia Orientalis* (Paris: 1907)

RAC: *Reallexikon für Antike und Christentum*, J.J. Dölger, ed.

RE: *Real-Encyclopädie der classischen Altertumswissenschaft*, C. Pauly, G.Wissowa, and W. Kroll, eds.

Rev. d'Ég.: *Revue d'Égyptologie*

RGRW: *Religions in the Graeco-Roman World*

RHR: *Revue de l'histoire des Religions*

RIASA: *Rivista dell'Istituto di Archeologia e Storia dell'Arte*

RIC: *The Roman Imperial Coinage*, I–X, C.H.V. Sutherland et al., eds.

SCI: *Studia Classica Israelica*

SGG I: *Sylloge gemmarum Gnosticarum*, I, A. Mastrocinque, ed.

SGG II: *Sylloge gemmarum Gnosticarum*, II, A. Mastrocinque, ed.

SNG: *Sylloge Nummorum Graecorum*

Suppl. Mag.: R.W. Daniel, F. Maltomini, *Supplementum Magicum*, I–II

TGF: *Tragicorum Graecorum fragmenta*, I–V (Göttingen: 1971–2004).

Vig Chr: *Vigiliae Christianae*

ZPE: *Zeitschrift für Papyrologie und Epigraphik*

# INTRODUCTION

# MAGICAL GEMS AS A DOCUMENTARY SOURCE FOR ANCIENT RELIGION

This book uses the iconography of magical gems as a documentary source for the knowledge of religions in the Roman empire. The compound of "magical gems" is the result of a modern choice, whereas antiquity did not know such a category. On the other hand, "amulets" (*periammata, phylakteria*) were known. Campbell Bonner entitled his very important handbook on this topic *Studies in Magical Amulets*.[1] He dealt also with bronze amulets of Late Antiquity and the Byzantine age, which are different from magical gems. In fact, amulets consisted mainly of pieces of papyrus or metal lamellae bearing prayers and other texts, as we can see by reading the recipes of magical papyri or *Hippiatricae*.

The category of "magical gems" was conceived in the Counter-Reformation intellectual environment to refer to iconographies of non-Olympian gods and odd images or inscriptions that appeared on carved gems. Scholars formulated various hypotheses.[2] Pirro Ligorio (Naples, 1513/14–Ferrara, 1583), in his work *Il libro cinquantesimo dell'antichità sopra delli significati dell'antichi intagli che si trovano con la imagine del scarabeo symbolo del sole*, says that these gems were inspired by the cults of Helios and Asklepios, and that they were amulets used against disease; Cesare Baronio (Sora, 1538–Rome, 1607), in his *Annales ecclesiastici* (Rome, 1588–1607), interpreted these gems as evidence of Gnosticism. This point of view was shared by Abraham van Gorle[3] (Antwerp, 1549– Delft, 1609) and Jean L'Heureux[4] (Gravelines, mid-sixteenth century–Aire en Artois, 1614). L'Heureux was a follower of François de Foix de Candale, bishop of Aire, a passionate researcher on Hermeticism. Jean Chiflet[5] (Besançon, 1612–Tournay, 1666) recognized gnostic and mithraic influences within the iconography of these gems. Athanasius Kircher (Geisa by Fulda, 1602–Rome, 1680), Lorenzo Pignoria (Padua, 1571–?), and Bernard de Montfaucon (Aube, 1655–Paris, 1741) were looking to magical gems for evidence of Egyptian religion.

In the century of Enlightenment, Luigi Bossi[6] supposed that magical gems were the artifacts of magicians, tricksters, and charlatans. In the

---

[1] C. Bonner, *Studies in Magical Amulets chiefly Graeco-Egyptian* (Ann Arbor: University of Michigan Press, 1950).

[2] On the opinion of learned scholars of the Renaissance and XVII–XVIIIth centuries, see A. Mastrocinque, ed., *Sylloge gemmarum Gnosticarum*, I (Roma: "Bollettino di Numismatica" Monografia 8.2.I, Istituto poligrafico e Zecca dello Stato, 2003), 127–33.

[3] *Dactyliotheca, seu annulorum sigillorumque promptuarium* (Nurnberg: 1601).

[4] J. Macarius, *Abraxas seu Apistopistus cui accedit* Jo. Chifletii, *Abraxas Proteus* (Antverpiae: 1657).

[5] In Macarius, *Abraxas*.

[6] L. Bossi, *Spiegazione di una raccolta di gemme* (Milan: 1795).

nineteenth century, the gnostic roots of magical gems were emphasized by Jacques Matter[7] and Charles W. King.[8] In 1914 Armand Delatte[9] founded the modern approach to magical gems thanks to comparisons made with magical papyri, and credited the magicians of the Roman Empire, inspired by the Egyptian religion, with the production of texts and images of magical gems. Starting from this date magical papyri and magical gems were studied together; *defixiones* and magical lamellae were added to this *corpus* to create the documentation of Imperial Age magical arts. Modern scholarship has been satisfied with this grouping of documents, which has been more or less accurately separated from texts and images that constitute what we regard as Classicity. In this way the Olympian gods were safe from contamination by magical iconography and texts. Adolf Furtwängler[10] excluded these gems from his work *Die antiken Gemmen* and from the National Archaeological Museum of Berlin, in favor of placement in the Egyptological Museum. The British Museum entrusted these embarrassing gems to the Medieval Department. Ulrich von Wilamowitz never took into account the magical papyri, which were considered an inferior product of antiquity.

In an about-face, during the middle of the twentieth century, Campbell Bonner and Alphonse Barb produced a series of seminal works in which they clarified the basis of the religious and theological speculation that underlay the iconographies and inscriptions of magical gems. These two authors recognized a plurality of religious streams that directed the engravers of gems. They discerned traces not only of Egyptian and Greek religion, but also speculations on Judaism.

Neither magical gems nor magical papyri and other types of magical documents were separated from ancient religions; on the contrary, they have to be held as precious evidence of religious streams that could not be classified as Olympic, classic, or Homeric. Neither were they evidence of true Egyptian or Jewish religions. Impurity, the contamination of what is deemed to be "a true religion" is the reason for singling out a magic document. One could also separate in the same way the theological works of Theurgy and Hermeticism, because they are inconsistent with Homer and Classicity.

The magical papyri of the Anastasi collection, gathered from a find near Egyptian Thebes, are a sort of litmus test for us to judge what is

---

[7] J. Matter, *Histoire critique du Gnosticisme* (Paris: Levrault, 1828); idem, *Une excursion gnostique en Italie*, (Paris: Levrault, 1852).

[8] C.W. King, *The Gnostics and their Remains* (London: Bell and Daldy, 1887).

[9] A. Delatte, "Études sur la magie grecque, III–IV", *Mus. Belge* 18 (1914): 5–96; idem, "Études sur la magie grecque, V, Akephalos theos", *Bulletin de Correspondance Hellénique* 38 (1914): 189–249.

[10] A. Furtwängler, *Die antiken Gemmen*, I–III (Leipzig: Giesecke & Devrient, 1900, reprint, Amsterdam-Osnabrück: Hakkert, 1964–1965).

magic and what is not, because everything in those papyri is deemed to be magical. In several recipes of those papyri the word "magic" is used to label a ritual or a religious attitude, but it is true that the owner of this library was interested in alchemy, theology, and literature.[11] This library is also a testimony of new forms of Egyptian religion in Imperial times,[12] in which the ancient local tradition was merged with the near-Eastern wisdom of the "Magi." The wisdom of these Magi was shaped in Persian or Jewish form.[13]

According to modern scholarship, Greco-Roman, that is, "classic" religion was only that of Homer and Cicero, and not that of Porphyry and Julian the Apostate, and even less that of the Hermetic texts or Chaldaean oracles. Classicity[14] stops when Oriental cults infect the Greco-Roman tradition. During the Roman Empire, the Jews and the Christians thought that the true Israel could not be where pagan or especially near-Eastern religious influences were present. The Christian apologists and heresiologists labeled as "magic" the doctrines that they recognized as Christian heresies.

This approach to non-Olympian religious traditions of the Imperial Age is embedded in the widespread opposition between magic and religion, which Christianity founded and first used against heretical Christians.[15] These heresies were mostly labeled as Gnosticism, which is a variety of Christianity infected by paganism and especially by Oriental religious elements.

In this book we will see that even characters of the ancient, classic Greek religion, such as Empousa, are present on the magical gems. Recent studies by Christopher Faraone have shown that many elements of Imperial Age magic arts were already present in Greek religion of the classical age. Hitherto the iconography of Empousa had not been recognized, neither was the iconography of Asklepios of Ascalon; consequently these iconographies had been labeled as "magical." In fact, they are characters of Attic religion and of a Palestinian pantheon, respectively. Our classification of these gems among the magical ones is not false, but only traditional. The god of Ascalon appeared odd, and because of that his gems became "magic." This is a tradition in the studies—a tradition that compels us to exclude

---

[11] See G. Fowden, *The Egyptian Hermes. A Historical Approach to the Late Pagan Mind* (Princeton: Princeton University Press, 1993).

[12] J. Dieleman, *Priests, Tongues, and Rites. The London–Leiden Magical Manuscripts and Translation in Egyptian Ritual (100–300 CE)*, Religions in the Graeco-Roman World 153 (Leiden: Brill, 2005).

[13] For such an approach to the topic see A. Mastrocinque, *From Jewish Magic to Gnosticism*, Studien und Texte zu Antike und Christentum 24 (Tübingen: Mohr-Siebeck, 2005).

[14] On the idea of "classicity," see S. Settis, *Futuro del "classico"* (Turin: Einaudi, 2004).

[15] H. Remus, "'Magic or Miracle'? Some Second-Century Instances," *Second Century* 2 (1982): 127–56; Mastrocinque, *From Jewish Magic*.

several votive gems[16] and other strange engravings from the Greco-Roman, Egyptian, Phoenician, Mesopotamian, or Sasanid gems, and to classify them in the mixed category of "magical" (or "gnostic") gems.

## THEOLOGY ON MAGICAL GEMS

Magical gems are very precious when attempting to understand particular religious speculations. We can recognize these speculations only when they are parallel to texts. These texts are found in the magical papyri or among the work of philosophers of Imperial times who were addicted to theology, astrology, and cosmology. In particular, many aspects of Kronos could be clarified thanks to magical gems. We will discover that this god was very important in theological multicultural speculations of Imperial times, and that believers resorted to him for love magic. His sexual features were the subject of important theological definitions, for example, the return to divine unity through the renunciation of sex. Kronos was he who generated many gods but finally gave up generation and resorted to contemplation of the supreme divine being.

The opposition of procreation through sex and generation through contemplation of God were features of many doctrines, such as Gnosticism, and the solar religion of Neoplatonism (one can think of Julian the Apostate). The magical gems bear witness to these speculations; in fact we find on them the emasculated or hermaphroditic Kronos, the god who obtains knowledge by contemplating the supreme and perfect god. We find also a creator god who is contemplating the form of the supreme god.

According to Plato, love causes the issue of the procreating substance when one sees Beauty. The famous discourse of Diotima in Plato's *Banquet* is as follows:

> Then love may be described generally as the love of the everlasting possession of the good . . . what is the manner of the pursuit? What are they doing who show all this eagerness and heat which is called love?...
>
> I will teach you: The object which they have in view is birth in beauty, whether of body or, soul . . .
>
> All men are bringing to the birth in their bodies and in their souls. There is a certain age at which human nature is desirous of procreation—procreation which must be in beauty and not in deformity; and this procreation is the union of man and woman, and is a divine thing . . .
>
> Beauty, then, is the Moira or the Eileithyia who presides at birth, and therefore, when approaching beauty, the conceiving power is propitious, and diffusive, and benign, and begets and bears fruit . . .

---

[16] See A. Mastrocinque, "Le gemme votive", in *Artisanats antiques d'Italie et de Gaule. Mélanges offerts à Maria Francesca Buonaiuto*, ed. J.-P.Brun, (Naples: Centre Jean Bérard, 2009), 53–65.

> For love, Socrates . . . is love of generation and of birth in beauty . . . .
> But why of generation? Because to the mortal creature, generation is a
> sort of eternity and immortality, and if, as has been already admitted,
> love is of the everlasting possession of the good, all men will necessarily
> desire immortality together with good: Wherefore love is of immortality.[17]

Plato is saying, through the words of the Delphic priestess Diotima,
that Beauty produces the creative act, that is, the issue of semen. This
statement was the starting point of a number of theological speculations
of the Imperial Age. The main idea that firmly rooted itself was the idea
that contemplation of the supreme god produced semen, which generated
the most splendid and divine children. The figure of the creator god himself
was shaped according to the theory of the contemplation of Beauty, that
is, of god, for this god created when contemplating. Therefore, the creator,
the Platonic Demiourgos, was believed to be inferior to the supreme god.

There were several religious communities in which rituals were performed so as to attain contemplation of god and consequently to issue
generative substances. Imitation of the creator god was a means of interfer-
ing with a divine power, and producing a substance that bore sparks of
supreme deities.[18]

Now we will see how Kronos, a cosmic god, gave up generation and
preferred contemplating the supreme Beauty. The first chapter of this book
will deal with the castration of Kronos and his transformation from a
begetter of cosmic gods to an asexual divine being. According to Greek
mythology, Ouranos was castrated by Kronos, but in many theological
speculations of the Imperial Age it was Kronos who was castrated.[19] For
Kronos is described as ἀρσενόθηλυς, "hermaphrodite," in the magical
papyri.[20] It is evident from many sources that Kronos was a very important
god in many theological systems of the Imperial Age, but the reasons
underlying this importance are still scarce, and in the following chapters
we will try to discover some of these reasons.

Kronos was also identified with important gods of other religions, such
as the Jewish and the Egyptian ones; in fact, he was identified with Sabaoth

---

[17] Plato, *Symposium* 206 A–207 A, B., *The Dialogues of Plato*, 4th ed., trans. B. Jowett, Oxford:
Clarendon Press, 1953). Plato, *Phaedrus* 250 B also dealt with the beatitude of souls who were
contemplating the world of Ideas before their descent into this world.

[18] See A.D. DeConick, "Conceiving Spirits: The Mystery of Valentinian Sex," in *Hidden Inter-
course. Eros and Sexuality in the History of Western Esotericism*, eds. J. Wouter Hanegraaff and J.J.
Kripal (Leiden: Brill, 2008), 23–48; A. Mastrocinque, *Des mystères de Mithra aux mystères de Jésus*,
Potsdamer Altertumswissenschaftliche Beiträge 26, (Stuttgart: Steiner, 2009), 102–8.

[19] Porphyr., *De antro Nymph.* 16.

[20] *Papyri Graecae Magicae* (henceforth quoted as *PGM*) IV, 3102; *PGM* VII, 607; cf. S. Eitrem,
"Kronos in der Magie," in *Mélanges Bidez*, I = *Annuaire de l'Institut de Philologie et d'Histoire
Orientales et Slaves* 2, (1934), 51–60.

and with Osiris.[21] These identifications resulted in the reshaping of our understanding of these three gods. But now it is time to consider the gems.

---

[21] On Sabaoth cf. A. Jacoby, "Das angebliche Eselkultus der Juden und Christen", *Archiv für Religionswissenschaft* 25 (1927): 271–82. On Osiris, see chapter 2.

# Chapter 1

## METAMORPHOSES OF KRONOS ON A GEM IN BOLOGNA

# THE OBVERSE SIDE OF THE GEM: KRONOS AND A RECIPE IN THE *KYRANIDES*

An important gem in the Civic Museum of Bologna[1] needs to be considered because it provides evidence of theological speculations of Near-Eastern theologists. The gem is a round obsidian (Figure 1.1) from about the 2nd century CE, which represents, on the obverse side, Kronos holding a sword-sickle (*harpe*) in his left hand and a mysterious object in his right; a globe is placed on top of his head. In another chapter we will deal with the reverse side, which depicts a boar above a leontocephalic snake. Obsidian

**Figure 1.1A**    Obsidian in the Civic Museum of Bologna (photograph by the author).

Reprinted with permission of the Civic Museum.

---

[1] A.R. Mandrioli, *La collezione di gemme del Museo Civico Archeologico di Bologna* (Bologna: Grafis, 1987), 134, no. 268. *SGG* II, Bo 6; cf., A. Mastrocinque, *Studi sul Mitraismo. Il Mitraismo e la magia* (Roma: Giorgio Bretschneider, 1998), 82–83 and fig. 19; idem, "Die Zauberkünste der Aphrodite. Magische Gemmen auf dem Diadem der Liebesgöttin (Kyranides I.10)" in *Otium. Festschrift für Volker Michael Strocka*, ed. T. Ganschow (Remshalden: Greiner, 2005), 223–31.

11

Figure 1.1B   Reverse side of the obsidian.

was chosen for this gem because it was the sacred stone of Kronos[2] and the gods who could be identified with him, such as Dispater.[3]   Another similar specimen, also carved on obsidian, is housed in the Vatican Library and was previously kept in the Borgia collection.[4]

Roy Kotansky[5] has published information about a gem in the collection of the J. Paul Getty Museum, in Santa Monica (Figure 1.2), which bears a similar iconography. He has identified this god with the Alexandrian Kronos, who is represented on several coins of the 2nd century AD (Figure

---

[2] *Kyanides* I, K 5, 3, ed. Dimitris Kaimakis; *PGM* CX, 6; *The Greek Magical Papyri in Translation*, ed. H.D. Betz (Chicago: University of Chicago Press, 1986, henceforth quoted as *GMPT*, 12); *PGM* CX, 6.

[3] Damigeron, 15 (64 Halleux-Schamp). According to Porphyry (Porphyrius, *Peri agalmaton* 2.1), black stones were chosen to represent the invisible gods.

[4] G. Zoega, "Catalogo del Museo Borgiano in Velletri", in *Documenti inediti per servire alla storia dei musei d'Italia*, a cura del Ministero della Pubblica Istruzione, III (Firenze-Roma: 1880), 479, n. 47.

[5] R. Kotansky, "Kronos and a new magical Inscription Formula on a Gem in the J.P. Getty Museum," *Ancient World* 3, no. 1 (1980): 29–32.

**Figure 1.2**  Jasper in the J. Paul Getty Museum.

Drawing by R. Kotansky.

1.3). Other images show Kronos holding the *harpe* in one hand and a small crocodile (Figure 1.4) or a gazelle in the other.[6] On yet another specimen, in the Skoluda collection,[7] he is clearly holding a crocodile (Figure 1.5). An obsidian in the Kelsey Museum in Ann Arbor[8] shows the same god (Kronos; Figure 1.6A) and, on the reverse side, Chnoubis in front of a fat pig (Figure 1.6B).

This version of Kronos represents the Egyptian Suchos, the crocodile-god, who was especially revered in Krokodilonpolis. During the Hellenistic and Roman period, the god Suchos was often represented with the iconography of Kronos (see Figure 1.4). This Suchos–Kronos was revered in many Egyptian sanctuaries. In Tebtynis he was called Σοκνεβτῦνις ὁ καὶ

[6] G. Dattari, *Monete imperiali greche. Numi Augustorum Alexandrini*, II (Cairo: Tipografia dell' Instituto Francese d'Archeologia Orientale, 1901), nos. 2684–5; cf. Figure 1.3 (bronze coin issued under Antoninus Pius, reverse side). A small bronze statue of the god holding the crocodile is kept in the Archaeological Museum at Florence: Fr. W. von Bissing, *Ägyptische Kultbilder der Ptolemaier- und Römerzeit* (Leipzig: Hinrichs, 1936), 27–8, fig.17; this author thinks that it represents Kronos identified as Suchos, the crocodile-god, and he quotes the evidence of Pap. Tebt. 302; cf. C. Dolzani, "Il dio Sobk" *Atti Accademia dei Lincei*, ser. VIII, 10 (1961), 223. Here, Figure 1.4 depicts the bronze Kronos-Suchos from the Museum of the Accademia Etrusca at Cortona. Thanks to the research of L. Kàkosy, "Das Krokodil als Symbol der Ewigkeit und der Zeit", *MDAI(K)* 20, 1956, 116 ff. = *Selected Papers (1956–73)*, Studia Aegyptiaca VII (Budapest: Archaeolingua, 1981), 113–118, part. 114, it has been clarified that in Egyptian culture the crocodile could represent Eternity; for this reason it was associated with Kronos, the god who was interpreted as time, *chronos*. Pseudo-Plutarchus, *De fluviis* 5.3 (where Cleanthes, the author of a work concerning the wars of gods, is quoted) narrates that Kronos, pursued by Zeus, transformed himself into a crocodile. The symbol of the gazelle could recall Seth, whose symbol was the oryx. The crocodile could also be a symbol of evil, and therefore could be linked to Seth.

[7] S. Michel, *Bunte Steine - Dunkle Bilder: "Magische Gemmen"* (Munich: Biering & Brinkmann, 2001), 120, no. 138; on the gem there is the Sisisrô *logos*.

[8] Ruthven collection no. 22; Bonner, *SMA*, 230 and 312, D 349.

**Figure 1.3** Alexandrian coin of Antonine age, representing the Egyptian Kronos.

Drawing by R. Kotansky.

**Figure 1.4** Small bronze statue of the Egyptian Kronos in Cortona, Museum of the Etruscan Academy and of the City of Cortona (photograph by the author).

Reprinted with permission of the Museum of the Etruscan Academy.

**Figure 1.5** Green and yellow/brown jasper in Hamburg, the Skoluda collection, representing Kronos–Suchos.

Photograph by S. Michel, reprinted with her permission.

Κρόνος: "Soknebtynis (i.e., Suchos lord of Tebtynis) *alias* Kronos."[9]
Indeed, the iconography of the gem in Bologna (see Figure 1.1) is very
similar to these other gems, but it does not show the god with the crocodile,
as on the stones depicted in Figures 1.3–1.6. The god on the gem in
Bologna may be associated with Egyptian doctrines, but he is also linked
to Near-Eastern theological doctrines.

The first book of the Lapidarium known as *Kyranides* (a stone book
of the 4th century CE, collecting more ancient works attributed to Hermes
Trismegistos and to Harpokration; the first book is called *Kyranìs*) presents, in alphabetical order, groups of one bird, one fish, one plant, and
one stone whose names begin with the same letter. These groupings were
supposed to share the same properties. This treatise had admittedly borrowed from Syrian[10] and Babylonian traditions.[11] Dealing with the letter
"K" a stone named *kinaidios*, "cinaedus,"[12] is presented, and the *Kyranìs*
(i.e., *Kyranides'* first book) says: "Although this stone is well known, the
*kinaidios* is scarcely recognized; it is called obsidian and is the property
of Kronos."[13] After that the treatise[14] explains how to make a magic gem:
"You should engrave on the obsidian an emasculated man, having his
sexual organs lying at his feet, his hands downward, and he himself looking

---

[9] G. Tallet, "Isis, the Crocodiles and the Mysteries of the Nile Floods: Interpretating a Scene
from Roman Egypt exhibited in the Egyptian Museum in Cairo (JE 30001)" in *Demeter, Isis, Vesta,
and Cybele. Studies in Greek and Roman Religion in Honour of Giulia Sfameni Gasparro*, eds. A.
Mastrocinque and C. Giuffrè Scibona, Potsdamer Altertumswissenschaftliche Beiträge 36 (Stuttgart:
Steiner, 2012), 139–163, part 145.

[10] I.1, 15, ed. Dimitris Kaimakis: βίβλος ἀπὸ Συρίας θεραπευτική.

[11] Cf. M. Wellmann, "Marcellus von Side als Arzt und die Koiranides des Hermes Trismegistos",
*Philologus* Suppl. XXVII.2 (Leipzig: Dieterich, 1934): 5 and n. 17; K. Alpers, "Untersuchungen zum
griechischen Physiologos und den Kyraniden", *Vestigia Bibliae* (Jb. d. deutsch. Bibel-Archivs Hamburg)
6 (1984): 13–88, part 22, maintained that the author of *Kyranides'* first book, entitled *Kyranìs*, was
Harpokration, pagan rhetor and poet of Julian the Apostate's milieu. He ascribes the 2nd and 3rd
books to another later author. Moreover he noticed that the *Kyranides* were often dependent on the
*Physiologos*, for Christian interpretations of natural phenomena are present in both treatises, but
they have no meaning in the *Kyranides*. The *Physiologus* could be dated to about 200 AD. However,
one must admit that no dependence on this Christian work is noticeable in *Kyranides'* first book,
which should be older than the others. Its organization has been traced back to the Seleucid Babylonian
tradition and therefore suggests a more recent date, maybe the 1st century CE, of its first recension;
see E. Weidner, "Gestirndarstellungen auf babylonischen Tontafeln", Sitzungsberichte der Österrei-
chischen Akademie der Wissenschaften. Phil.-hist. Klasse 254 (1967), 30. According to Ps. Plutarchus,
*De fluviis* 21, Koiranos (who represents a *varia*—and *deterior*—*lectio* of Kyranos in the *Kyranides*)
is the father of Polyidos, the seer.

[12] I.10, 62–65, ed. Dimitris Kaimakis; cf. the Latin translation: *Textes latins et vieux français
relatifs aux Cyranides*, L. Delatte, ed. (Liège-Paris: Les Belles Lettres, 1942), 55–61. On amulets that
are described in *Kyranides'* first book: M. Waegeman, *Amulet and Alphabet—Magical Amulets in
the first Book of Cyranides* (Amsterdam: Gieben, 1986) (at 79–85 the letter K is dealt with, but
not the problems of Kronos and obsidian). On Aphrodite's *kestos himas*: see Mastrocinque, "Die
Zauberkünste der Aphrodite" (see note 1).

[13] 63, ed. Dimitris Kaimakis.

[14] 65, ed. Dimitris Kaimakis.

**Figure 1.6A**    Obsidian in the Kelsey Museum, Ann Arbor, representing Kronos–Suchos (photograph by the author).

Reprinted with the permission of the Kelsey Museum.

down towards his genitals. Aphrodite is to be engraved behind him, shoulder to shoulder, and she is gazing at him." Such an amulet made its wearers impotent or effeminate. This amulet was concealed in the center, on the inner side of Aphrodite's leather ribbon, the κεστὸς ἱμάς. On the outer side stood 12 gems, which produced different love incantations. This

**Figure 1.6B    Reverse side of the obsidian representing Kronos–Suchos.**

ribbon was known to Homer,[15] who thought it was a ribbon or a rope with many piercings, which concealed all magical love charms. In the Hellenistic and Roman world this ribbon became a diadem or a crown on Aphrodite's head that was decorated with many magical gems.[16] The *Kyranìs* says that the gem of Kronos was endowed with the most terrible incantation. As we have seen, it is Kronos, not Ouranos, who was supposed to be castrated; the magical papyri define him as a "hermaphrodite." Additionally, the power of his gem fits well with his features according

---

[15] *Iliad*, XIV, 214–217; this passage is very rich in myths that depended on Near-Eastern sources (Tethys and Okeanos were Hera and Zeus's parents; at first they loved each other, but later they divorced, in exactly the same way as Tiamat and Apsu, according to the Babylonian *Enuma Elish*; moreover Aphrodite's leather ribbon is similar to Mesopotamian ribbons empowered by knots or also semi-precious stones to produce love incantations or to receive the favor of the gods). See C. A. Faraone, "Aphrodite's KESTOS and apples for Atalanta: Aphrodisiacs," *Phoenix* 44 (1990): 219–43; idem, *Ancient Greek Love Magic* (Cambridge, Mass.: Harvard University Press, 1999), 97–110. Aphrodite's *kestòs himas* (pierced ribbon) is also mentioned in a love spell: D. Jordan, "A Love Charm with Verses," *ZPE* 72 (1988), 245–59.

[16] On the Egyptian and Near-Eastern iconography of Aphrodite with such a crown: Mastrocinque, "Die Zauberkünste" (quoted in n. 1).

to the mythology of magical papyri. These beliefs were supported by a passage of Homer's *Iliad*[17]:

> I (scil. Hera) am faring to visit the limits of the all-nurturing earth, and Oceanus, from whom the gods are sprung, and mother Tethys, even them that lovingly nursed and cherished me in their halls, when they had taken me from Rhea, what time Zeus, whose voice is borne afar, thrust Cronos down to dwell beneath earth and the unresting sea. Them am I faring to visit, and will loose for them their endless strife, since now for a long time's space they hold aloof one from the other from the marriage-bed and from love, for that wrath hath come upon their hearts.

The gem dates from the second century, and, in any case, no later than the third century AD. This is proof that in the middle years of the Imperial Age the topics of the *Kyranis* were well known.

If we take a look at the Bologna gem, it is evident that Kronos is holding his genitals in his right hand.[18] He holds his genitals on the gem in the Getty Museum as well. The Museum für Kunst und Gewerbe in Hamburg contains a third gem (a green and brown/yellow stone) with Kronos's image.[19] On this gem, the god stands over his hooked sword, the *harpe*, and holds the same object seen in the Bologna specimen. On the reverse side, the Sisisrô *logos* is legible and a small cynocephalic monkey riding the back of a lion is visible.

Two yellow and green jaspers in the Skoluda collection (Hamburg)[20] (Figures 1.7A and B) and in the J. Paul Getty Museum[21] show Kronos and, on the other side, the monkey riding on the back of a lion, surrounded by the Sisisrô *logos*. It is difficult to recognize what Kronos holds in these specimens. A green and yellow jasper kept in the Cabinet des Médailles[22] (Figure 1.8) shows the same image—a monkey riding the lion; on the obverse side, the Sisisrô *logos* suggests that the gem is of the same series, and that the god represented is Kronos. Here he resembles Harpokrates (i.e., Horus, the child); his right hand rests near his mouth. Nevertheless, there is no doubt that this is Kronos because a *charakter* supports him—a character similar to the hieroglyph that represents water.[23]

---

[17] Homer, *Iliad*, XIV, 200–208, A.T. Murray, trans.

[18] A heliotrope intaglio in Braunschweig Museum (*AGDS* III Braunschweig, no. 78; F. Baratte, *LIMC* VIII, Supplement no. 18) shows Saturnus holding a very strange sickle; it is similar to a phallus.

[19] M. Schlüter, G. Platz-Horster, and P. Zazoff, *AGDS* IV, no. 78 (1975).

[20] Michel, *Bunte Steine-Magische Gemmen*, no. 138.

[21] S. Michel, *Die magischen Gemmen* (Berlin: Akademie Verlag, 2004), 322, plate 59.1 and color plate III.8.

[22] Delatte, Derchain, no. 201.

[23] Delatte, Derchain, no. 151. Kronos and water will be discussed in subsequent paragraphs, and especially in footnote 62.

**Figure 1.7A** Green and yellow jasper in Hamburg, the Skoluda collection, representing the Egyptian Kronos and a monkey riding on the back of a lion.

Photograph by S. Michel, reprinted with her permission.

The prayer in the fourth magical papyrus, which follows[24] an appeal to "the snake, the lion, fire, water, and the tree," is devoted to Horus Harpokrates, the lord of the sun. The prayer to "the snake, the lion, fire, water, and the tree" is offered to Kronos, who is identified with the sea god Proteus, as we will see in the chapter devoted to the reverse side of the gem in Bologna.

Kronos and Harpokrates were invoked in the same prayer. There is no contradiction in this: Harpokrates was the shape the sun took during the day, whereas Kronos–Osiris was its image at night. Evidently the author of the spell maintained that Kronos/Harpokrates was a single god with various shapes. This fact could help to explain the shape of the Kronos on the gems, who is making the gesture common to Harpokrates.

The Egyptian Suchos–Kronos was worshipped with a similar and younger god. A recent contribution by Gaëlle Tallet observes:

---

[24] *PGM* IV, 985 ff.

**Figure 1.7B   Reverse side.**

In the Fayum, the perennity of kingship and the regeneration of the cosmos was fulfilled by two crocodiles, a young one and an aging one, deemed to be a form of Osiris born again as Horus, and of the evening sun regenerated during the night. These crocodiles clearly belong to two different generations: as Ra is often depicted as a child in the morning, as a mature grown up at its zenith, and as an old man in the evening, and as Osiris and Horus are father and son, I think the two faces of the god with a crocodile, beardless when young and bearded when aging, are not of the same age and refer to different moments of a common cycle. As a matter of fact, in Tebtynis, Soknebtynis, alias Kronos, shared his shrine with a younger crocodile, Sobek-Ra-Horakhty, and in Roman Soknopaiou

**Figure 1.8A**   Green and yellow jasper in the Cabinet des Médailles, Paris, representing the Egyptian Kronos and a monkey riding on the back of a lion (photograph by the author).

Reprinted with permission of the Cabinet des Médailles.

> Nesos, the two crocodile gods, Soknopaios and Soknopiai(i)s, were probably a son and a father—the young one, Soknopaios, could be depicted as a hieracocephalous crocodile.[25]

Therefore, we deduce that this form of Kronos represents the younger god, similar to Horus.

## THE EMASCULATED KRONOS

The *Kyranides* passage about obsidian as well as the doctrine that inspired the design of the Bologna gem, derive from speculations by Hellenistic

---

[25] Tallet, "Isis, the Crocodiles and the Mysteries of the Nile Floods," (quoted in n. 9) 149–50.

**Figure 1.8B** Reverse side.

Chaldaeans. In fact, a late cuneiform text[26] ascribes to each zodiac sign a temple, a plant, and a stone. The "castrated one's stone" is attributed to Capricorn. According to ancient astrology, Kronos's "home" was in Capricorn.[27] It is important to note that obsidian was the stone used for castration as well as for circumcision.[28]

---

[26] E. Weidner, "Gestirndarstellungen auf babylonischen Tontafeln", Sitzungsberichte der Öster-reichischen Akademie der Wissenschaften. Phil.-hist. Klasse 254 (1967): 30; G. Pettinato, *La scrittura celeste. La nascita dell'astrologia in Mesopotamia* (Milan: Mondadori, 1998), 114.

[27] Servius, *ad Georgicas* I.336; Firmicus Maternus, *Mathesis* III.1; Ptolemaeus, *Tetrabiblos* I.19; Numenius, fr. 31 Des Places.

[28] Epiphanius, *De gemmis* 95 (*The old Georgian Version and the Fragments of the Armenian Version*, by R. P. Blake and *the Coptic-Sahidic Fragments*, by H. De Vis (London: Christophers, 1934), 193. The *Bible* (*Ioshua* 5.2) spoke generically of stone knives. In the *Pirkê de Rabbi Eliezer* (G. Fiedlander, ed. New York: 1971, 212, § XXIX), they were made of silex. On circumcision as an attenuation or substitution for emasculation cf. H. Graillot, *Le culte de Cybèle, Mère des dieux, à Rome et dans l'empire romain* (Paris: Fontemoing, 1912), 293. Pseudo-Plutarchus, *de fluviis* 10 describes a stone that was similar to iron, called *machaira* (sword); when it was found in the Marsyas river by men who performed the mysteries of Kybele, it made them go mad. Therefore it is possible that it was a stone with which they emasculated themselves. The same author, at § 12, quotes the *autoglyphos* stone of the Sagaris river, which bore the image of Kybele. The Galli, who found it, always wore it.

**Figure 1.9A** Hematite in the Kunsthistorisches Museum, Vienna, representing an emasculated god or priest lusted after by a goddess or a woman.

Reprinted with permission of the Kunsthistorisches Museum.

It is likely that a gem in the Kunsthistorisches Museum in Vienna[29] (Figure 1.9) shows the scene that is described in the *Kyranìs*. It is a hematite on which one can see a standing man, wearing a tunic, possibly his hair is feminine; another person, probably a woman, is kneeling behind him. The inscription on the reverse side is certainly a love charm: Νιχαροπληξ διχαίως, that is, "stimulate the favor![30] With good reason!" It is unclear whether this man has his feet on the left or on the right side. A foot is visible on the side of the kneeling woman, but on the other side one could say that there are two slightly diverging feet. If we recognize in the gem the iconography alluded to in the *Kyranìs*, the diverging feet should be

---

[29] E. Zwierlein-Diehl, *Die antiken Gemmen des Kunsthistorischen Museums in Wien*, III (München: Prestel, 1991), no. 2211.

[30] Νειχαροπληξ is the anagram of πλῆξον χάριν; cf. A. A. Barb, rev. of Delatte-Derchain, *Gnomon* 41 (1969), 305. The adverb διχαίως is typical of the gems that depict Eros' punishment by Psyche: cf. A. Merlin, "Intaille représentant le châtiment d'Éros", in *Mélanges Maspéro*, II (Mémoires de l'Institut Français d'Archéologie Orientale du Caire 66. Paris: Imprimerie de l'Institut Français, 1934–1937,) 131–36. This scene recalls the rituals of the Syrian temple of Bambyke-Hierapolis, where the castrated priests wore women's garments and were desired by women: Lucianus, *De dea Syria* 19–27; in particular, 22. The Christian writer Rufinus (*Historia ecclesiastica* II.25) says that a priest of the Alexandrian Kronos convinced several women that the god wanted them to sleep in the temple; he appeared, disguised as Kronos, and had sexual intercourse with them. It is possible that this scarcely reliable account testifies to rituals similar to those of Bambyke.

Figure 1.9B   Reverse side.

interpreted rather as the fallen genitals of the god. He is therefore looking at the genitals and turning his head back to despise the woman gazing at him.

## THE REVERSE SIDE

Our attention now turns to the iconography on the reverse side of the Bologna gem, Figure 1.1B. Here a boar stands over a leontocephalic snake whose head is surrounded by rays, like Chnoubis. As I have already argued,[31] this animal iconography represented the metamorphoses of Kronos. In fact, the Vatican Mythographer (an anonymous writer of a Vatican manuscript of mythology, in three books)[32] reports that the head

---

[31] *Studi sul Mitraismo*, 82–83, see n.283. This iconography had been formerly interpreted as that of Horus fighting with Seth (D. Wortmann, "Kosmogonie und Nilflut", *Bonner Jahrbücher* 166 (1966): 91; cf. also C. Bonner, *Studies in Magical Amulets Chiefly Graeco-Egyptian* (Ann Arbor: University of Michigan Press, 1950), 30–31; Ph. Derchain, "Intailles magiques du Musée de Numismatique d'Athènes," *Chr. d'Eg.* 39 (1964), 190. An interpretation of the castrated boar as Seth, the sterile god, could have been (if this is the case) only a secondary one.

[32] Mythogr. Vatican. III (1.8, 155–56), ed. Bode = F. Cumont, *Textes et monuments figurés relatifs aux mystères de Mithra*, II (Bruxelles: Lamertin, 1898), 53–54. In the *Second Book of Jeu* (*Koptisch-gnostische Schriften*, I, ed. Carl Schmidt, 207) an evil god is described, whose head was that of a boar with the body of a lion. According to the diagram of the Ophites (in Origenes, *Contra Celsum* VI.30), Michael was placed in the circle of Saturnus and had the form of a lion.

of Saturnus (the Latin name for Kronos) had different forms according to the seasons, namely, those of a snake, a lion, and a boar. Moreover, the sacred stone of Kronos was called "snake's stone." [33] On the other hand, the boar was the animal that killed both Adonis and Attis.[34] Attis is the emasculated hero of the Phrygian mysteries. According to Ovid,[35] Adonis had been castrated by a boar.

Decans that have the form of Kronos were supposed to present the features of a boar.[36] The identification of Kronos with the boar is reported in the great magical papyrus of Paris,[37] where it is explained how to make a phylactery in order to force Kronos to give oracles. This phylactery bore the image of Zeus with the sickle; and was made of a rib of a castrated black boar, which was surely the image of Kronos. In the same instruction Kronos is appealed to as the hermaphrodite (ἀρσενόθηλυς) and is attracted by the practitioner with salt, a product of the sea. Kronos delivered his oracles in the same manner used by Menelaos to attract and force Proteus to deliver oracular answers. We will discuss this type of divination in detail in chapter 2. Now we will discover why Kronos should be conceived as a boar. The use of the lion as an image for Kronos is more difficult to explain. However, monuments found in Roman Africa[38] show Saturnus accompanied by a lion.

Homer's *Odyssey*[39] tells the story of the capture of Proteus—the Old Man of the Sea. Proteus's daughter Eidothea explains that this hidden and omniscient god can transform himself into water or fire. When caught by

---

[33] *Kyranides* I.10, 63 ed. Dimitris Kaimakis; Ps. Callisth., *Historia Alexandri* (recensio A) I.4.5, p. 33, ed. Wilhelm Kroll. The description of the *Draconitis lapis* (stone of serpent, serpentine) by Plinius, *Naturalis historia* XXXVII.158 is less explicit. He says that it was translucent and was placed in the head of snakes, cf. Tertullianus, *De cultu feminarum* 1.6. According to Philostratus, *Vita Apollonii* III.8, a stone in the head of snakes was bright with many colors (cf. Orphei, *Lithikà kerygmata*, 49). It was used to make Gyge's ring, which gave invisibility to its owner (Plato, *Respublica* 359 B ff. and Phot., *Lexikon*, s.v. Κανδαύλου γυνή). A snake's stone is mentioned in the *Bible* (I *Kings* 1.9), where it is said that Adonias wanted to become king and was sacrificed with this stone.

[34] Pausanias VII.17.9 (from Hermesianax of Colophon, 4th cent. BC); cf. Herodotus I. 36–43 (on the death of Atys, Croesus' son, killed by a boar).

[35] Ovidius, *Metamorphoses* X.715; cf. *Amores* III.9.16; other authors maintain that the boar killed him: Apollodorus III.14.4; Bion 1.7-8 (*Bucolici Graeci*, ed. A. S. F. Gow, Oxford: Clarendon Press, 1992).

[36] H.G. Gundel, *Dekane und Dekansternbilder*, Studien der Bibliothek Warburg 19 (Hamburg: Augustin, 1936, reprint Darmstadt: Wissenschaftliche Buchgesellschaft, 1969), 365, 380.

[37] *PGM* IV, 3115–3119. On this passage of this papyrus: R. Merkelbach and M. Totti, *Abrasax. Ausgewählte Papyri religiösen und magischen Inhalts*, I, Papyrologica Coloniensia 17.1 (Opladen: Westdeutscher Verlag, 1990), 3–10; J.L. Calvo Martìnez, "El Himno χαῖρε δράχων del papiro parisino. Ediciòn crìtica con introducciòn y comentario," *MHNH* 4 (2004): 265–78.

[38] F. Baratte, Kronos/Saturnus, *LIMC* VIII Supplement 70 (2009): nos. 70 and 86.

[39] Homer *Odyssey*, IV.418 e 456–458. On the theological interpretations of Homer in Medio- and Neoplatonism, see R. Lamberton, *Homer Theologian* (Berkeley: University of California Press, 1986), 17, 26–27. Lamberton discusses Iamblichus, *Theologia arithetica* 7.20–23 and Proclus, *in Rempublicam* 1.112.28-9 e, according to which Proteus had in himself all the forms of all things.

Menelaos, Proteus transforms into a lion, a snake, a panther, a large boar, then turns himself into water and finally into a tree.

A prayer to the sun in a spell found in the great magical Papyrus of Paris, which merges Egyptian and Jewish–Gnostic elements, is to be recited in front of the rising sun and later in front of a lamp; it begins thus:

> Hail, Snake and invincible lion, natural sources of fire. And hail, clear water and lofty-leafed tree![40]

Identification between Kronos and a sea god[41] is predictable because the Babylonian god Ea, god of sea water and of magic, was called "Kronos" by the Greeks; Marduk, on the other hand, was called "Zeus." According to the Peratae (a "Gnostic" sect), Kronos was identified with the biblical god; he was also a hermaphroditic god of watery substances.[42] The Pythagoreans believed the sea was formed out of Kronos's tears.[43] The later Neoplatonists gave Kronos and his planet sovereignty over water.[44] In the next chapter we will analyze the identification of Kronos with Osiris, who was another god of water, particularly of the flooding of the Nile.

The multicultural magic used during the Imperial Age endorsed the myth of Proteus, as stated by Pliny the Elder[45]: "if, indeed, we are willing to grant that his [viz. Homer's] accounts of Proteus and of the songs of the Sirens are to be understood in this sense [viz. as evidence of magic arts]." The Gnostic sect of the Naassenes believed Proteus was the god who moved the heavenly pole. They identified him with the Phrygian god

---

[40] *PGM* IV, 939–941; a quotation is to be singled out: δένδρεον ὑψιπέτηλον: *PGM* IV, 941 = Homer, *Odyssey*, IV.458.

[41] F. Baratte, Kronos/Saturnus, *LIMC* VIII Supplement. (2009), no. 116

[42] Hippolytus, *Refutatio haeresium* V.17–19.

[43] Plutarchus, *De Iside et Osiride* 32 = 364 A (this author, in a previous passage, attributed salt to Typhon). The hieroglyph °vw°, "water," is also a *charakter* of Kronos: *Hygromanteia Salomonis*: CCAG, VIII.2, 158 and pl. I. On Aphrodite and salt: S.-T. Teodorsson, "An Epithet of Aphrodite," *Glotta* 66 (1988): 135–36 (the adjective ἀλειοία is to be read ἁλιοία: "[goddess] of salt").

[44] Proclus, *in Timaeum* II.48; Macrobius, *Somnium Scipionis* I.11.8, according to which, the heavenly (*ourania*) water was entrusted to Kronos, whereas Hermes controlled the ethereal water; see F. Lasserre, "Abrégé inédit du Commentaire de Posidonios au Timée de Platon (P gen. Inv.203)" in *Protagora, Antifonte, Posidonio, Aristotele. Saggi su frammenti inediti e nuove testimonianze da papiri*, eds. F. Adorno, F. Decleva Caizzi, F. Lasserre, and F. Vendruscolo (Accad. Toscana "La Colombaria", Studi 83) (Firenze: Olschki, 1986) 104 and footnote 29; W. Hübner, "Zum Planetenfragment des Sudines, P. env. inv. 203," *ZPE* 73 (1988): 35–36.

[45] Plinius, *Naturalis historia* XXX.6.1: *siquidem Protea et Sirenum cantus apud eum non aliter intellegi volunt*; translated by J. Bostock and H.T. Riley (London: Taylor and Francis, 1855). For Proteus as a *lekanomantis*: Tzetzes, *Chiliades* II. 626–40. For a possible ancient Egyptian tradition of Eidothea's betrayal of her father, see P. Gilbert, "Eidothéé, Théonoé et les temples de Medinet Habou," *Nouvelle Clio* 10–12 (1958–1962): 178–83. On magic in the Homeric narrative: S. Lonsdale, "Protean forms and disguise in Odyssey 4," *Lexis* 2 (1988): 165–78; see also R. Piettre, "Les comptes de Protée," *Métis* 8 nos.1–2 (1993): 129–46.

Polykarpos.[46] This god was prophetic, proteiform, and—at least partially—serpentine. To remind us of these identifications, the constellation of Draco (Latin for "snake") sits on the cosmic pole. In the mithraic mysteries the leontocephalic god Frugifer was worshipped;[47] his head corresponds to that of the leontocephalic Aiôn, who is represented on the top of the cosmic globe in the fresco of the Barberini mithreum.[48] His name, Frugifer, seems to correspond to Polykarpos. The leontocephalic god of Mithraism was also a hyperouranic god—he had features of Chronos (Time) and Herakles—whose cosmic manifestation was that of Kronos.[49]

The hermaphroditic nature of the highest god is a feature that occurs not only in Gnosticism and other doctrines followed during the Imperial Age. As we will see in chapter 3, hermaphrodism is also present in very different cultural environments, such as Indian or Egyptian religions.[50] The god on the gem, moreover, is emasculated, not hermaphroditic. In the Greek *Theogonies*, Kronos was the father of many gods. Evidently his castration happened after his theogonic phase. The Naassenes applied the term *arsenòthelys*, "hermaphrodite," to Attis, the emasculated god.[51] Also it is possible that a complete refusal of sex was supposed to be equivalent to divine hermaphroditism, and that each religious stream thought of the refusal of sex by the old god differently.

## MANY FORMS OF KRONOS AND OF THE JEWISH GOD

The reverse side of the Bologna gem shows a triple animal form of the god: a lion, a snake, and a boar. This triple nature is also seen on the gem

---

[46] Hippolytus, *Refutatio haeresium* V.8.35. The Naassenes doctrines were often shared by the Peratae. On the other hand it is noteworthy that Simon Magus took Helene into the center of his doctrine. According to the Greek myth, Helene was related to Proteus and Menelaos.

[47] Arnobius, *adversus nationes* VI.10: "*Inter deos videmus vestros leonis torvissimam faciem mero oblitam minio et nomine frugifero nuncupari.*" On Frugifer (who could be identified with Saturnus) cf. A. Blomart, "Frugifer: une divinité mithriaque léontocéphale décrite par Arnobe", *RHR* 210 (1993): 5–25.

[48] M.J. Vermaseren, *Corpus inscriptionum et monumentorum religionis Mithriacae*, II (The Hague: Nijhoff, 1960), 390.

[49] Just as Mithra was the hyperouranic sun, Helios was the cosmic one. On those topics see A. Mastrocinque, *Des mystères de Mithra aux mystères de Jésus*, Potsdamer Altertumswissenschaftliche Beiträge 26 (Stuttgart: Steiner, 2009), 57–70.

[50] J. Zandee, "Der Androgyne Gott in Ägypten. Ein Erscheinungsbild des Weltschöpfers", in *Religion im Erbe Ägyptens. Beiträge zur spätantiken Religionsgeschichte zu Ehren von Alexander Böhlig*, ed. M. Görg (Wiesbaden: Harrassowitz, 1988), 240–78. The ancients themselves were often uncertain of the hermaphroditism and asexuality of the supreme gods: Lactantius, *De ave Phoenice* 163; cf. G. Quispel, "Gnosis and the New Sayings of Jesus," *Eranos Jahrbb.* 38 (1969): 201–10 = *Gnostic Studies*, II (Istanbul: Nederlands Historisch-Archaeologisch Instituut in het Nabije Oosten, 1975), 180–209, part 202–3.

[51] Hippolytus, *Refutatio haeresium* V.7.

in the J. Paul Getty Museum. The gem combines the image of Kronos holding a *harpe*[52] with the names Ἰάω Cαβαὼθ Ἀδωναῖ, οἱ τρεῖς οἱ μεγάλοι. Perhaps these three names correspond to three forms or manifestations of Kronos. During the age of Tacitus, Saturnus (i.e., Kronos) was identified with the Jewish god.[53] The Jewish god had three forms or features in addition to his own; Macrobius in fact reports a famous oracle of Apollo Klarios,[54] who, when questioned about Iaô's nature, replied: "You must know that Iaô is the most great among the gods, who is Hades in winter, Zeus when spring comes, Helios in summer, and the mighty Iaô in autumn." Three Hebrew names, Iaô Sabaoth Adonai, correspond to three animal features: a snake, a lion, and a boar. The Jewish god as a snake and a lion was known to the Gnostic sects,[55] especially in the compound form of Chnoumis (or Chnoubis), the lionheaded snake.[56] Indeed, the snake and the lion merge into one form: Chnoubis. There is no specific reason for such an iconography on the gems of Kronos. The only possible explanation is that Chnoubis is considered to be lord of the Nile flood and of every watery substance.[57] A gem depicts this god with the hieroglyph that signifies water;[58] the same hieroglyph accompanies Harpokrates–Kronos on the gems in the Cabinet des Médailles (see Fig. 1.8). Pagan magi, as we have seen, shared the idea of a great god in the form of a lion and a snake: "Hail, Snake and invincible lion," was the prayer to the prophetic god.[59] The bishop Epiphanius testifies[60] that some Gnostic thinkers claimed that the Jewish god took the form of a pig. This strange belief does not depend on the famous prohibition of pork,[61] but on the boar's feature of Kronos–Yahweh. The manifestation of the great prophetic

---

[52] Kotansky, *Kronos.*

[53] Tacitus, *Historiae* V.2.4.

[54] Macrob. I.18.19–20; cf. P. Mastandrea, *Un neoplatonico latino. Cornelio Labeone* (Leiden: Brill, 1979), 159–169.

[55] On the god as a lion, see: Origenes, *Contra Celsum* VI.30–31; cf. *The Nature of Archons* 94; *Origin of the world* 100; *Apocryphon Iohannis* 10: Synopsis 25 (*Coptic Gnostic Library*, II.1, 60–61); *Pistis Sophia*, I.31–32, 39; H. M. Jackson, *The Lion Becomes Man. The Gnostic Leontomorphic Creator and the Platonic Tradition* (Atlanta: Scholars Press, 1985); J. E. Fossum, *The Name of God and the Angel of Lord* (Tübingen: Mohr-Siebeck, 1985), 321–329. On the god as a snake, see *Acta Thomas* 32 (*Acta Apost. Apocr.*,) II.2, M. Bonnet, ed. (Leipzig: Mendelssohn, 1903; reprint Darmstadt: Wissenschaftliche Buchgesellschaft, 1959), 149; Epiphan., *Panar.* XXVI.10.8 (I, 296, ed. Karl Holl); this idea was shared by the Samaritan Saduqal, cf. J. Fossum, "Sects and Movements," in *The Samaritans* ed. A. D. Crown, (Tübingen: Mohr-Siebeck, 1989), 336. In *Numeri* 21.6-7 the Seraphim were shaped in the form of snakes.

[56] *Apocryphon Iohannis* 10: Synopsis 25 (*Coptic Gnostic Library*, II.1, 60–61).

[57] See A. Mastrocinque, *From Jewish Magic to Gnosticism*, Studien und Texte zu Antike und Christentum 24 (Tübingen: Mohr Siebeck, 2005), § 20–21.

[58] Deltte, Derchain, no. 352; on this hieroglyph on a gem depicting Kronos: see above, footnote 43.

[59] PGM IV, 939–40; *Anecdota Atheniensia*, ed. Delatte, 41 e 117–8: ὁ λέων Cαβαώθ.

[60] *Panarion* XXVII.12 (I, 288 ed. by Karl Holl).

[61] Cf. A. Jacoby, "Der angebliche Eselkult der Juden und Christen", *ARW* 25 (1928): 268.

and proteiform god as a tree could also be relevant to the Jewish god, who appeared as a thorny bush on Mount Sinai.

The gems in Bologna, Hamburg, and Santa Monica suggest the value of identifying Kronos with the Jewish god.[62] Varro, in the time of Caesar, wrote that the Chaldeans studied the nature of the Hebrew god in their secret writings.[63] The Greeks and Romans wanted to identify such a mysterious god with an Olympian god so as to understand his nature, and Kronos was featured in an appropriate manner for that identification. He had been removed from Olympus and confined in distant lands. A myth was told, according to which Kronos left Crete, after the victory of Zeus, and was followed by the Jews.[64] This points to the idea that Kronos was the god of the Jews—proof of such an identification[65] resided in the etymology of Sabaoth as the god of the number seven, *sheba'* in Hebrew.[66] Consequently, the seventh planetary heaven, Saturnus, was that of Kronos–

---

[62] On the importance of that identification, see A. Barb, "St. Zacharias the Prophet and Martyr," *JWCI* 11 (1948): 64–5.

[63] Lydus, *de mensibus* IV 53 = Varro, *Rerum divinarum libri* I, fr. 17 Cardauns; cf. also Augustinus, *Confessiones* IX.10.24. See G. Scholem, "Über eine Formel in den koptisch-gnostischen Schriften und ihren jüdischen Ursprung", *ZNW* 30, (1931): 170 ff.; E. Norden, "Jahve und Moses in hellenistischer Theologie", in *Kleine Schriften zum klassischen Altertum*, (Berlin: de Gruyter, 1966), 282–5; I. Gruenwald, *Apocalyptic and Merkavah Mysticism* (Leiden-Köln: Ithamar, 1980), 145; E. Bickerman, "The Altars of Gentiles. A Note on the Jewish «Ius sacrum»," in *Studies in Jewish and Christian History*, II (Leiden: Brill, 1980), 324–46, part. 337–42; Mastrocinque, *From Jewish Magic*, 47–50.

[64] Tacitus, *Historiae* V.2.3.

[65] About which cf. Tacitus, *Historiae* V.2.4: "We are told that the rest of the seventh day was adopted, because this day brought with it a termination of their toils; after a while the charm of indolence beguiled them into also giving up the seventh year to inaction. However, others say that it is an observance in honour of Saturn, either from the primitive elements of their faith which have been transmitted from the Idaei, who are said to have shared the flight of that God, and to have founded the race, or from the circumstance that of the seven stars which rule the destinies of men Saturn moves in the highest orbit and with the mightiest power, and that many of the heavenly bodies complete their revolutions and courses in multiples of seven." See also Origenes, *Contra Celsum* VI.31 (Ialdabaoth has the form of a lion and a *sympatheia* with the Phainon planet, that is, with Saturn).

[66] Jacoby, *Der angebliche Eselkult*, 268. John Lydus (*de mensibus* IV.38) writes: "The Chaldeans call Dionysos Iaô, in Phoenician language (. . .); furthermore he is often called Sabaoth, because he is placed over the seven spheres; this signifies that he is the creator. Than he adds: "creator Sabaoth: this is indeed the name of the demiurgical number by the Phoenicians." Commentaries of the *Bible* construe the name of Sabaoth as "week," or as "fullness," "completeness"; cf. Hieronymus, *ad Jeremiam* 5.24 (*in Hebraeo enim scriptum est Sabaoth, quod pro ambiguitate verbi, et septimanas significat, et plenitudinem*). Translations of the *Bible* by Aquila and Theodotion have: πλησμονάς (=*plenitudo*, "completeness," "fullness"). Cf. also Lactantius, *Institutiones* VII.14: *hic est autem dies sabbati, qui lingua Hebraeorum a numero nomen accepit, unde septenarius numerus legitimus ac plenus est*. If we take into account this concept of "fullness," we must remember that Sabaoth was identified as Kronos, and that Plato (*Cratylus* 396 B) suggested interpreting "Kronos" as *koros nous*, "full mind"; similarly St Augustine (*De consolatio evangelica* I.23.35) defined Saturnus as *satur nous*, "full mind." On those etymologies, cf. J.-G. Préaux, "Saturne à l'ouroboros", in *Hommages à Waldemar Deonna*, Collection Latomus 28 (Bruxelles: Latomus, 1957), 394–410, part. 397–403.

Sabaoth.[67] The seventh day of the week was considered sacred to Saturnus (Saturday, identified with Sabaoth) and corresponded to the Sabbat.

The later Neoplatonist Damascius[68] states that Pythagoreans and Phoenicians assigned to Kronos the number seven, which encapsulates unity and triplicity. Indeed, again we are faced with doctrines and speculations that were shared by Gnostic thinkers, magicians, and learned pagans. Similar cases are frequent. The gems testify to speculations on the asexual, hermaphroditic, and trifold nature of the Jewish god. One can remember the long disquisition of Hippolytos, in the fifth book of his *Refutatio*, on Naassene theories: To explain the mysterious sexuality of their supreme god, they resorted to the myths of Attis. It is evident that the iconography of the gems in Bologna, Hamburg, and Santa Monica trace back to Chaldean speculations on the Jewish god and speculations of Gnostic thinkers. Plotinus[69] testified that Gnostic thinkers attended his school and that many of them persisted in their beliefs. Forms of cultural osmosis occurred between pagans and Gnostics. Nevertheless the iconography of Kronos and the comparison with the *Kyranìs* leads one to assign the gem in Bologna to pagan environments.[70]

## SARAPIS AND THE JEWISH GOD

The identification of the Jewish god with Kronos runs parallel to Kronos's identification with Sarapis (i.e., the Hellenistic form of Osiris), a god whose image was often equated with Yahweh. In fact, Sarapis was invoked with names or formulae of the Jewish god. For example, we read beside him μέγα τὸ ὄνομα τοῦ κυρίου Σέραπις (=Σεράπιδος), or εἷς Ζεὺς Σάραπις ἅγιον ὄνομα[71] or Ὕψιστος Σάραπις.[72] Several gems represent Sarapis

---

[67] In the *Nature of Archons* 95 (*Coptic Gnostic Library*, II.2, 255) Sabaoth refused the actions of his father Ialdabaoth, and therefore was shifted to the seventh heaven. Here, he obtained a power which was seven times greater than the Archons of the seven planetary heavens, and seven Archangels were recruited into his service. The Phariseans called the planet of Saturn χωχὲβ σαβέθ (Epiphanius, *Panarion* XV.2; I, 211, ed. Karl Holl), a name which could easily be linked to Sabaoth.

[68] *Dubitationes* 265, II, 131, ed. Ruelle (this work is commonly called also *de principiis*).

[69] *Enneades* II, 10, 125, ed. Bréhier.

[70] It is worth remembering that R. P. Casey, in "Naassenes and Ophites," *Journal of Theological Studies* 27 (1926): 374–87, part. 387, suggested searching at Hierapolis for the origin of the Naassene Gnostic movement. They were the worshippers of the snake, which was thought of as the image of Christ; according to Casey, from Naassene doctrine sprang the sects of the Peratae, the Sethians, and the Ophites. It is known that Naassenes greatly valued the myth of Attis and Magna Mater.

[71] Respectively: Bonner, *SMA*, p. 322, D 398; Delatte-Derchain, no. 101; C. W. King, *The Gnostics and their Remains* (London: Bell and Daldy, 1887), p. 172; other examples are found in E. Le Blant, *750 inscriptions de pierres gravées*, Mém. Acad. Inscr. XXXVI (Paris: Klincksieck, 1898), no. 202 ff.

[72] Cf. S. Perea Yébenes, *El sello de Dios (Σφραγὶς Θεοῦ)* (Madrid: Signifer Libros, 2000), 45–46.

**Figure 1.10**    Green and red-stained jasper in the Skoluda collection, Hamburg, representing Sarapis on a boat.

Photograph by S. Michel, reprinted with her permission.

and bear the inscription Ἀλδαβαῖμ,[73] which is an equivalent of Ἰαλδαβαῖμ or Ἰαλδαβαώθ, the name the Gnostics used to call the biblical creator. These gems represent Sarapis on his boat (Figure 1.10), with a scarab flying from his head. The inscription refers to the scarab, for a series of gems show the scarab with the inscription Ἰαλδαθιαὶν ξιφιδίῳ χνημιδίῳ.[74] The scarab took the form of the rising sun, the young sun, and Ialdabaôth represents the Semitic word *yeled, yalda*, "young," "child," "son."[75] Other specimens with the scarab bear the name Ἰάω, Iaô, that is, Yahweh.[76] Two passages in the magical papyri[77] consider Aldabaoth as the creator god. Two others[78] say that Aldabiaim is the Egyptian name for the sun, and it is equivalent to Abrasax.

---

[73] A. Delatte, "Etudes sur la magie grecque, III-IV", *Mus. Belge* 18 (1914): 53; H. Philipp, *Mira et Magica: Gemmen im Ägyptischen Museum der staatlichen Museen*, (Mainz: Philipp von Zabern, 1986), n. 78; Michel, *Bunte Steine*, no. 34 (here Fig. 1.9); see also the fragmentary gem edited by Bonner, *SMA* , no. 256, plate I.20 (inscription ABAIM). Cf. King, *Gnostics*, 249. It it also possible that this name alluded to Aldemios or Aldos, two names of the god Marnas, a local "Zeus" worshipped at Gaza: Etym. M. 58.20. According to *PGM* XIII, 152–3 Aldabiaeim was the Egyptian name of the sun; in *PGM* XIII, 971 the divine name Αλδαζαω was borrowed from a book by Moses. On those gems and the identification of the scarab with Ialdabaoth, see A. Mastrocinque, "Serapide e le gemme aquileiesi", in *Il fulgore delle gemme. Aquileia e la glittica di età ellenistica e romana*, eds. G. Sena Chiesa and E. Gagetti (Trieste: Editreg, 2009), 101–9.

[74] For example, *IGLS* IV, 1292 = R. Mouterde, "Objects magiques. Recueil S. Ayvaz," *MUB* 25 (1942-43), 109, no. 10; Bonner, *SMA*, 268, D 93; Philipp, *Mira et Magica*, no. 118; Michel, *British Museum*, no. 101; *SGG* I, 128.

[75] Mastrocinque, *From Jewish Magic*, 77. See the Nag Hammadi codex in the *Origin of the World* 10 (NHC II, 5, 100, 10; 42; *Coptic Gnostic Library*, II.5, p. 35): «Child, pass through to here», whose equivalent is «*yalda baôth*».

[76] F.M. Schwartz, J.H.Schwartz, "Engraved Gems in the Collection of the American Numismatic Society I. Ancient Magical Amulets," *ANSMN* 24 (1979), 172, no. 28; Michel, *British Museum*, no. 93.

[77] *PGM* XIII, 462; 596.

[78] *PGM* XIII, 84 and 152–3.

The well-known acclamation εἷς Ζεὺς Σάραπις,[79] found on gems and other monuments, could hardly be completely unrelated to the Jewish idea of one single god, even though "one" often refers to important pagan gods or goddesses.[80] Ptolemy the First promoted the creation of the cult of Sarapis. He required all his subjects to be followers of this cult. The Jewish tradition claims that Ptolemy manifested his devotion to the god in Jerusalem.[81] According to the *Historia Augusta*,[82] during the time of Hadrian Christians in Egypt venerated Sarapis. There are no valid reasons to claim that the *Historia Augusta* is wrong in this respect, since at the time of Hadrian the word "Christians" was also used to designate Gnostic Christians. In chapter 2 we will deal further with the identification of Sarapis or Osiris with Kronos.

## THE INSCRIPTION

On the reverse side of the Bologna gem there is a problematic inscription, found within two circles, which says: οχλοβα ζαραχω βαριχαμμω βαλ / ξι κηβκ χαμασι. We will now consider similar inscriptions found on other gems.

1. The inscription on the Bologna gem is best compared with an agate gem in the Cabinet des Médailles,[83] which shows *charakteres* encircled by an *ouroboros* snake, and, on the other side, the inscription: σισιρω σισιφερμου Αμουωρ Αβρασαξ αχλοβαρα. ζαραχω βαριχαμμω σιχηρ.

---

[79] Cf. Bonner, *SMA*, 174–6.

[80] L. Di Segni, "«εἷς Ζεὺς Σάραπις»" in Palestinian Inscriptions" *SCI* 13 (1994): 94–115.

[81] *Aristeas' Letter to Philokrates* 16; Iosephus, *Antiquitates Iudaicae* XI.1 ff.; these texts indeed testify to the apologetic aim of philhellene Jews, and therefore they are not to be read without caution. A controversial passage of the *Historia Augusta* (*Vita Saturnini* 8) asserts that Christians worshipped Sarapis in Egypt in the age of Hadrian. Cf. W. Schmid, "Die Koexistenz von Sarapiskult und Christentum im Hadrianbrief bei Vopiscus", in *Bonner Historia Augusta-Colloquium 1964–1965* (Bonn: Habelt, 1966), 153–184; R. Syme, *Ipse ille patriarcha*, in *Bonner Historia Augusta-Colloquium 1966–1967* (Bonn: Habelt, 1968), 119–30; A. Baldini, *L'epistola pseudoadrianea nella Vita di Saturnino*, in *Historiae Augustae Colloquium Maceratense*, eds. G. Bonamente and G. Paci (Bari: Edipuglia, 1995), 35–56.

[82] *Vita Saturnini* 8. It is usually thought that a late legend underlined the interpretation of the graffito of an *ankh*, which is similar to a cross, and was found on a wall of the Serapeum, as proof of the common religious basis of Christianity and the Sarapis religion: Socrates, *Historia ecclesiastica* V 17 (GCS Sokrates, 290–91 Hansen); Sozomenus, *Historia ecclesiastica* VII 15, 10 (GCS Sozomenus 321 Bidez, Hansen); cf. F. Thelamon, *Païens et chrétiens au IVe siècle: l'apport de l'"Histoire ecclésiastique" de Rufin d'Aquilée* (Paris: Éditions Augustiniennes, 1981), 267–73. On the authenticity of Hadrian's letter in the Vita Saturnini cf. esp. F. Dornseiff, "Der Hadrianbrief in der frühbyzantinischen Historia Augusta", in *Aus der Byzantinischen Arbeit in der Deutschen Demokratischen Republik*, ed. J. Irmscher, I (Berlin: Deutsche Akademie der Wissenschaften, 1957), 39–45.

[83] Delatte-Derchain, no. 511.

**Figure 1.11** Obsidian in the Skoluda collection, Hamburg, representing a pig and a snake, with the SISISRO spell.

Photograph by S. Michel, reprinted with her permission.

Two obsidian gems in the Vatican Library (previously in the Borgia collection), representing Kronos and a boar with a snake, have the following inscriptions:

2. αβαζα σισιρρω σισαω σισιφαραχω βαηχαμμ[84] and

3. [Αβρ]ασαξ οχας [_ _ _]ω εαιειχον ρισισρω σισιφερμου χνουω.[85]

4. A green jasper in a private collection, representing the boar and the leontocephalic snake,[86] has the same *logos*: σισισρω σισιφερμο Χμουωρ Αβρασιξ ιβηχ.

5. The same iconography is on an obsidian in the Skoluda collection[87] (Figure 1.11), and the inscription: ρεμελλο αμμιμελωθ σισισρω σισιφερμου χλεουωρ Αβρασαξ.

6. The same iconography is on the already-quoted obsidian in the Kelsey Museum (see Figure 1.6).[88] On the other side of the gem sits Kronos (similar to Sarapis) on his throne, which is placed on the back of a crocodile. An inscription is cut on the bevel: Χμουωρ Αβρασ[αξ σι] σισρω σισιφερμου.

7. An obsidian in the Cabinet des Médailles[89] (Figure 1.12) bears the same iconography and the inscription [.]ΚΛΟΒΑ[...]ΡΑΧΟΡΡΙ [ΒΑΡΙ]ΧΑΜΜΟ ΣΙΞΙ[.]ΗΒΚ ΣΙΣΙΣΡΩ ΣΙΣΙΩ [ΑΒΡ]ΑΣΑΞ ΣΙΣΙΦΕΡΜΟΥ ΝΧΝΟ[...]

8. On a green-yellow jasper in the Cabinet des Médailles[90] (see Figure 1.8), representing Kronos pointing his index finger to his mouth (like Harpokrates), one reads: σισισρω σισιφορμχλου Χνουωρ Αβρασαξ.

---

[84] G. Zoega, *Catalogo del Museo Borgiano in Velletri*, in: *Documenti inediti per servire alla storia dei musei d'Italia*, a cura del Ministero Pubbl. Istr., III (Firenze-Roma: Bencini, 1880), 479, n. 47.

[85] Zoega, 436, n. 16.

[86] Bonner, *SMA*, 229-230, D 348.

[87] Michel, *Bunte Steine-Magische Gemmen*, no. 139.

[88] Bonner, *SMA*, D 349.

[89] Delatte, Derchain, no. 216

[90] Delatte, Derchain, no. 201.

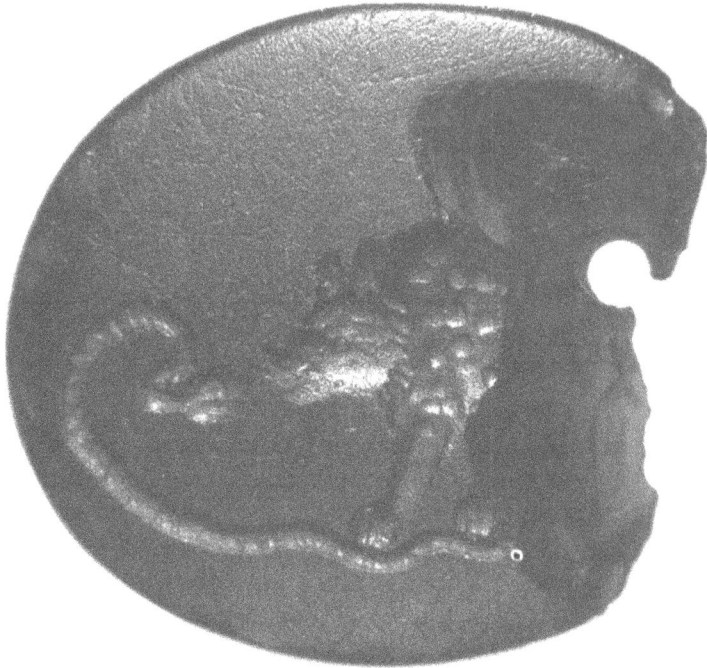

**Figure 1.12A** Obsidian in the Cabinet des Médailles, Paris, representing a pig and a snake, with the SISISRO spell (photograph by the author).

Reprinted with the permission of the Cabinet des Médailles.

9. A serpentine in the British Museum[91] shows Kronos holding *harpe* and thunderbolt (?), standing on a lion, bearing this inscription: σισιωσισιφερμουανου.ρχν. On the reverse side there is Hekate standing on a corpse, accompanied by an inscription that speaks of the stomach, the father, and the good.

10. An intaglio showing an elephant (Figure 1.13) bears this inscription: (σ)ισισρω (σι)σιφερμ(ου) Χμουωρ Α(βρα)σαξ Οχλοβαρω βαρ (ιχ)αμμω σιχηρ.[92]

11. In an erotic charm inscribed on papyrus[93] one can read: σισισρω σισιφερμου Χμουωρ Ἀρουηρ Αβρασαξ Φνουνοβοηλ Οχλοβαζαραχωα βαριχαμω, and it is explained that this *logos* could be abbreviated to Βαχαμ χηβχ.

[91] Michel, *British Museum*, no. 296.

[92] *SGG* I, 382.

[93] *Suppl. Mag.* I, 42, ll.49–50, in the commentary by Daniel and Maltomini other occurrences of the *logos* are quoted.

**Figure 1.12B**  Reverse side.

**Figure 1.13**  Drawing from Montfaucon, representing an elephant and the SISISRO spell.

Reprinted with permission from *L'antiquité expliquée*, Suppl. II, 1724, 213, plate 55, 5.

Now we will attempt to explain the meaning of the spell inscribed on the Bologna gem and present comparisons with similar magical texts. The first words are Egyptian.

Σισρω (Sisrô) signifies "son of the ram." Ram, Σρῶ, was the form of the sun during the sunset. Σερφουθ μουι σρω were indeed the forms of the sun during the day: lotus, lion, ram. Three gods corresponded to these forms: Rê, Khepri, Atum.[94] However, Simone Michel[95] correctly maintains that Σισι Σρω (Sisi Srô) are two Decans of Capricorn,[96] and that Capricorn was Saturnus's astrological "home."[97] We will address the astrological features of the gems of Kronos in the section "The Monkey on the Back of a Lion."

Ζαραχω occurs in a magical papyrus,[98] where it is the name of the Aiôn always restored to life.

Χνουωρ ends with the name of Horus: Ὡρ.

Ἀρουηρ is Egyptian, and signifies "the great Horus." We notice again that the gem in the Cabinet des Médailles represents Kronos making the gesture of Harpokrates, that is, as a young god with his left forefinger in his mouth. Harouêr is also a Decan in the *Apocryphon of John* 17.[99]

Αβρασαξ, or Abrasax, is the omnipresent divine name; its numerical value is 365.

Φνουν is Egyptian, and signifies "the abyss."

Βαριχαμ(μ)ω is made up of Bari and Chamô. Bari was pronounced "Vari," and correseponded to Jari, the North-Arabian name of the moon, which was present also in the name of the emperor Heliogabalus: Varius.[100] Chamô is equivalent to Χααμου, the Arabian name of Kore.[101]

---

[94] M.-L.Ryhiner, "A propos des trigrammes panthéistes", *Rev. d'Ég.* 29, (1977): 125–136; cf. R. Merkelbach and M. Totti, *Abrasax*, I (Opladen: 1990), 101.

[95] S. Michel-von Dungern, "Studies on Magical Amulets in the British Museum," in *Gems of Heaven. Recent Research on Engraved Gemstones in Late Antiquity c. AD 200-600*, eds. Ch. Entwistle and N. Adams (Proceedings of the conference, London 28–31 May). British Museum Research Publication 177, (London: The British Museum, 2011), 85; cf. *Supplementum magicum*, I, 150; A.v. Lieven, "Die dritte Reihe der Dekane", *ARG* 2, (2000): 32.

[96] The second and the third Decans of Capricorn are, according to Hephaistion I.1 (I, 25, ed. David Pingree), Σρω and Ἰσρω. On the names of those Decans, cf. J.-H.Abry, "Les noms des Décans dans la tradition hermétique", in *Le tablettes astrologiques de Grand (Vosges) et l'astrologie en Gaule romain, Actes de la Table-ronde du 18 mars 1992 organisée au Centre d'Études Romaines et Gallo-romaines de l'Université Lyon III*, ed. J.H. Abry (Lyon: Centre d'Études Romaines et Gallo-Romaines, Diffusion De Boccard, 1993), 77–78.

[97] See, e.g., Hephaistion I.1; I, 24, ed. David Pingree.

[98] *PGM* VII, 511. In the papyrus edited by R. W. Daniel, "Some ΦΥΛΑΚΤΗΡΙΑ," *ZPE* 25, 1977, 153, we find . . . βαλοχρα Θαμρα ζαραχθω.

[99] Synopsis 47 (*Coptic Gnostic Library*, II.1, 105).

[100] Cf. F. Hiller von Gärtringen, "Syrische Gottheiten auf einem Altar aus Cordoba", *ARW* 22, (1924): 117; R. Turcan, *Eliogabalo e il culto del sole*, Italian transl. (Genova: ECIG, 1991), 11. In *PGM* IV, 2269: βαριδούχε is a name of the moon goddess.

[101] Epiphanius, *Panarion* LI.22.11 (II, 286, ed. Karl Holl). With good reason Holl, in his critical apparatus, refuses the correction from Χααμον to Χααβου (which could allow the writing of an untrustworthy protohistory of the Kaaba). Nevertheless such a correction finds agreement; cf., e.g., T. Fahd, *Le panthéon de l'Arabie centrale à la veille de l'Hégire* (Paris: Geuthner, 1968), 169, 204. The form βαριχαα Κμῆφ should be noted on a lamella from Amisos, which dates back to the beginning of the Imperial Age: R. Kotansky, *Greek Magical Amulet*, I (Opladen: 1994), no. 36. If βαρι(χαα) is equal to βαρι(χαμω), we can suppose that the author of the lamella combined Bari with Kmeph, a name of the Egyptian creator god and of the Alexandrian Agathodaimon (on which: H. J. Thissen, "ΚΜΗΦ- Ein verkannter Gott", *ZPE* 112 [1996]: 153-60). On the cult of Kore among the Samaritans, who identified her with Iephtes' daughter (*Judges* 11.39): Epiphanius, *Panarion* LV.1.9; LXXVIII.23.6 (II, 325 and III, 473, ed. Karl Holl).

Οχλοβαζαρα occurs, in the form Οχλοβαζαρω, in a *defixio* from Egypt,[102] along with Χνουωρ Αβρασαξ Φνουνοβοηλ. The form Οχλο-βαζαρα is linked here to the Μασχελλι *logos* and seems to refer to the goddess Brimô. On another gem the same magical *vox* is inscribed close to the monogram of Christ.[103] Gormakaiochlabar is a Decan in the *Apocryphon of John* 16.[104] Βαλ occurs on a gem with the "seal of Solomo" (i.e., a series of *charakteres* that were supposed to represent the name of god): Εαβαὼθ Βῆλ Βάλ.[105] Βῆλ Βάλ and Βòλ were names of the supreme heavenly god that were used at Palmyra.[106] Βελβελ is a Decan in the *Testament of Solomo* 18, and Βαλβηλ is his name in the *Apocryphon of John* 16.[107]

As in the Egyptian *defixio*, other occurrences of the *logos* referred to a male and female divinity: the god of darkness and afterlife (Sarapis or Osiris, who is also called Eulamô, and Kronos), and the goddess of the dead (Brimô and Hekate on the *defixio*). The aim of the *defixio* was to restrain anger, and a recent study by Christopher Faraone[108] has shown that Kronos and the Titans were invoked in binding spells to restrain or dispel anger.

To conclude this section, we can say that Kronos on the Bologna gem is a Near-Eastern god, who became the object of sophisticated theological speculation. This late-antique Kronos is a synthesis of several features of the Greek god, of the Egyptian Suchos–Kronos, of Yahweh, and of Osiris-Sarapis. He was meant to be emasculated and asexual. His realm is the remote region of the afterlife and of darkness, which is reflected in the dark color of the obsidian also used to represent him. Figure 1.14 shows another obsidian gem that represents the Egyptian or Near-Eastern Kronos,

---

[102] J.G. Gager, *Curse Tablets and binding Spells* (New York: 1992), no. 115. Cf. also *PGM* XII, 167: Οχλοβαραχω.

[103] E. Le Blant, *750 inscriptions de pierres gravées*, in Mém. Acad. Inscr. XXXVI (Paris: Klinck-sieck, 1898), no. 251.

[104] Synopsis 44 (*Coptic Gnostic Library*, II.1, 99). J.F. Quack, "Dekane und Gliedervergottung: altägyptische Traditionen im Apokryphon Johannis", *JbAC* 38 (1995): 117 supposes he is the 3rd Decan of Fishes, Olachm. In the Nag Hammadi cod. IV.25, 19 the name is cut into three parts, so that the original text was Γόρμα καὶ Οχλαβαρ.

[105] G. Bevilacqua, *Antiche iscrizioni augurali e magiche dai codici di Girolamo Amati* (Roma: Quasar, 1991), 25–27.

[106] H.J.W. Drijvers, "After Life and Funerary Symbolism in Palmyrene Religion," in *La soterio-logia dei culti orientali nell'impero romano*, eds. U. Bianchi and M. J. Vermaseren (Leiden: Brill, 1982), 213.

[107] Synopsis 43 (*Coptic Gnostic Library*, II.1, 97); he created the fingers of Adam's left hand. See also *PGM* IV, 1010; Βελβαλι: *PGM* XIII, 75; Philipp, *Mira et Magica*, no. 141. See Quack, "Dekane und Gliedervergottung", 115.

[108] C.A. Faraone, "Kronos and the Titans as Powerful Ancestors: A Case Study of the Greek Gods in Later Magical Spells" in *The Gods of Ancient Greece*, eds. J. N. Bremmer and A. Erskine (Edinburgh: Edinburgh University Press, 2010), 388–405.

**Figure 1.14**  Obsidian in the Cabinet des Médailles, Paris, representing an Egyptian (or Near-Eastern) Kronos (photograph by the author).

Reprinted with the permission of the Cabinet des Médailles.

accompanied by magical words and symbols.[109] An obsidian axe was also used as a medium for a Mithraic magical instrument, on both sides of which Mithra and Kronos are represented in the center of 28 *charakteres* (Figure 1.15).[110]

## THE MONKEY ON THE BACK OF A LION

We now focus on a few gems that represent Kronos, bear the logos *sisisrô*, and show on the reverse side a cynocephalic monkey (or ape) riding on the back of a lion. These specimens are carved most often on yellow and green jasper:

1. One is in the Museum für Kunst und Gewerbe in Hamburg;[111]
2. a second is kept in the Cabinet des Médailles[112] (see Figure 1.8);
3. a third is in the J. Paul Getty Museum;[113]
4. another is kept in the Skoluda collection[114] (see Figure 1.7);
5. another is a chert with veins of chalcedony, published by Bonner;[115]
6. only one is represented on a hematite gem, which is kept in the Museum of Cairo, and represents the monkey on the back of the lion and, on the obverse side, bears the inscription: IAω AEω IAEω.[116]

This astonishing iconography has been brilliantly explained by Simone Michel.[117] She noticed that the monkey is the sign of the Egyptian *dôdecaôros,* which corresponds to Capricorn, the "home" of Saturnus. The *dôdecaôros* is a series of animal symbols that indicate the forms of the sun during its daily journey.[118] According to another theory,[119] it indicates

---

[109] Delatte, Derchain, no. 421. A black glass gem, published by R. Veymiers, "Ἵλεως τῷ φοροῦντι. *Sérapis sur les gemmes et les bijoux antiques* (Brussels: Académie Royale de Belgique, 2009), 300, no. III.D7, represents the Egyptian Kronos standing on a crocodile and holding a scepter with a hook; on the reverse side the name of Sabaoth is engraved.

[110] A. Mastrocinque, *Studi sul Mitraismo. Il Mitraismo e la magia* (Roma: Giorgio Bretschneider, 1998), chapters VI–IX.

[111] M. Schlüter, G. Platz-Horster, P. Zazoff, *AGDS IV* (Wiesbaden: Prestel, 1975), no. 78 = S. Michel, *Die magischen Gemmen* (Berlin: Akademie Verlag 2004), 322, color plate III.8.

[112] Delatte, Derchain, no. 201.

[113] Michel, *Die magischen Gemmen,* 322, plate 59.1 and color plate III.8.

[114] Michel, *Bunte Steine-Magische Gemmen,* no. 138.

[115] Bonner, *SMA,* 294, D 248.

[116] L. Barry, "Notice sur quelques pierres gnostiques", *ASAE* 7 (1906): 247, no. 8.

[117] S. Michel-von Dungern, "Studies on Magical Amulets in the British Museum," in *'Gems of Heaven'. Recent Research on Engraved Gemstones in Late Antiquity c. AD 200-600,* eds. Ch. Entwistle and N. Adams (proceedings of the conference London, London 28–31 May). British Museum Research Publication 177, (London: The British Museum, 2011), 85.

[118] *PGM* III. 300–30.

[119] F. Boll, C. Bezold, and W. Gundel, *Sternglaube und Sterndeutung* (4th ed., Leipzig: Teubner, 1931), 57.

**Figure 1.15A**  Obsidian-carved axe representing Mithra and Kronos in the collection of Federico Zeri.

Reproduced with permission of Federico Zeri.

**Figure 1.15B**   Reverse side.

**Figure 1.16**   The Tabula Daressy, representing the Egyptian dôdecaôros.

Reprinted from F. Boll, *Sphaera* (Leipzig: Teubner, 1903), chap. 13.

a selection of the 28 stops of the moon in the constellations. The forms of these signs are known thanks to a poetic version written by John Camateros (12th century) of the treatise of Teukros the Babylonian, which was also described by Antiochos and Rhetorios.[120] The 12 animals of Teukros correspond to those on the Tabula Bianchini and on the Tabula depicted by Daressy[121] (Figure 1.16). Many of them are engraved on several gems all around Harpokrates or the Phoenix.[122] These signs were:

---

[120] See F. Boll, *Sphaera* (Leipzig: Teubner, 1903), chap. 13; W. Gundel, *Neue astrologische Texte des Hermes Trismegistos*, Abhandlungen Bayerischen Akademie Wiss. Neue Folge 12, 1936, 229 ff.

[121] A complete account of the iconography of the *dôdecaôros* is found in Boll, *Sphaera*.

[122] S. Michel, *Die magischen Gemmen* (Berlin: Akademie Verlag, 2004), 66–67.

| Ram: cat | Crab: scarab | Balance: goat | Capricorn: baboon |
|----------|--------------|---------------|-------------------|
| Bull: dog | Lion: donkey | Scorpion: bull | Aquarius: ibis |
| Twins: snake | Virgin: lion | Bowman: falcon | Fishes: crocodile |

It is possible that the lion is a manifestation of the sun. On the back of this lion stood the monkey, a symbol of Capricorn. Kronos was depicted in his astrological home, Capricorn, which corresponded to the winter solstice. The period represented by this Sign is one of long nights and cold temperatures, during which the sun is considered an aged god.

So far we have reported the theory of Simone Michel. Now we take another step forward. Cassius Dio,[123] when describing the vices of the emperor Heliogabalus (who was also allegedly called Sardanapalus), mentions a strange ritual:

> I will not describe the barbaric chants which Sardanapalus, together with his mother and grandmother, chanted to Elagabalus, or the secret sacrifices that he offered to him, slaying boys and using charms, in fact actually shutting up alive in the god's temple a lion, a monkey, and a snake, and throwing in among them human genitals, and practising other unholy rites, while he invariably wore innumerable amulets.

Cassius Dio, as well as the *Historia Augusta*, underlines the sexual extravagances of Heliogabalus, who, among his numerous oddities, behaved like an emasculated priest[124] and planned to cut off his genitals altogether.[125] The gems depicting an emasculated Kronos and a monkey on the back of a lion may have been inspired by the same doctrines that inspired the ritual of the emperor. This latter was born in Emesa, where Helios was worshipped. Moreover he could read the most secret Egyptian holy books; in fact Septimius Severus, in 199 AD, "took away from practically all the sanctuaries every book that he could find containing any secret lore."[126] The doctrines of the great temple of Emesa could hardly contradict those of other religious centers or perhaps those of magical papyri. It is indeed possible that the sexual behavior of Heliogabalus suggests that he was aware of the theology of Kronos, the castrated or hermaphrodite god, and to his animal avatars.

The belief that Kronos was emasculated was not shared by every province of the Roman Empire; it was typical of magical documents, which have no sure geographical roots. The emasculated gods were typical of

---

[123] Cassius Dio LXXIX.11.3 (III, p. 464 Boissevain); transl. Earnest Cary (Cassius Dio, IX, Loeb Classical Library, Cambridge, Mass: Harvard University Press, 1927), on the basis of the version by Herbert Baldwin Foster.

[124] *Scriptores Historiae Augustae, Heliogabalus* 7.

[125] Cassius Dio LXXX.11.

[126] Cassius Dio LXXVI.13.

Anatolia and Northern Syria. Kronos with the crocodile was typical of Egypt, whereas Kronos with the boar was not Egyptian, but rather a Near-Eastern feature of his cult. In any case, these forms of mythology and the cults associated with it were not the product of the western, Latin regions of the empire.

## THE PURPOSE OF THE KRONOS GEMS

The gems of Kronos were, or were also, love amulets. The specimen in Bologna was placed at the center of Aphrodite's crown and was supposed to be the most powerful love charm, for it could make a man change his sexual behavior. Also the recipe in *PGM IV* has been mentioned, in which a phylactery had to be used to threaten Kronos: it was a rib of a castrated black boar, engraved with the image of Zeus holding a sickle. Therefore a castrated black boar is an image associated with Kronos, and amulets created from black stones with Kronos's image could favor only an asexual life. A fragment from the philosopher Damascius indicates that the Chaldeans were able to make "chastity rings."[127] We can only wonder whether such rings had something to do with the mythology of Kronos.

A surprising fact is that a few transparent stones are engraved with the image of a male boar copulating with a wild sow[128] (Figure 1.17). Apparently these gems represent the opposite of the Kronos black gems: intense heterosexual activity, fecundity, luminous gems, versus asexual behavior, disregard for female beings, sterility, black gems. In fact, boars and pigs are very fecund animals. The legend of Aeneas and the 30 piglets is a very famous example of this.

In addition to the series engraved on black, green/yellow, and transparent stones, there is another series, most often engraved on red or yellow jasper, which represents a boar holding a bull's head or something else in its mouth. The details of these gems are as follows:

1. The yellow jasper in the Numismatic Museum in Athens[129] shows the boar with an unidentified object in its mouth and the inscription τὸ τῆς φιλίας ΜΟΥΙΩΡ. The last word is constructed from μουι: "lion,"

---

[127] Damascius, *Vitae Isidori reliquiae*, ed. Clemens Zintzen, fr.111, p. 87.

[128] T. Gesztelyi, *Antike Gemmen im Ungarischen Nationalmuseum* (Budapest: Ungarisches Nationalmuseum, 2000, no. 257 (crystal rock; here, Fig. 1.17); E. Brandt, A. Krug, W. Gercke, and E. Schmidt, *AGDS* I, *München*, (München: Prestel, 1972), no. 2896 (aquamarine). I am indebted to T. Gesztelyi for the photograph of this gem.

[129] Ph. Derchain, "Intailles magiques du Musée de Numismatique d'Athènes", *Chr.d'Eg.* 39, no. 18 (1964): 189–90.

**Figure 1.17A**  Crystal rock representing a boar copulating with a wild sow and a dog-headed (?) divinity riding on a sheep or a ram, National Museum, Budapest.

Reprinted courtesy of Prof. Tamás Gesztelyi.

and Ὧρ: "Horus." But it is possible that it is a mistake for ΜΟΥΙΣΡΩ: μουι "lion," σρῶ "ram."

2. Another yellow jasper, in The Hague Museum,[130] shows the animal holding a bull's head and the inscription: ΜΟΥΙΣΡΩ.

3. An almost identical specimen is kept in the Cabinet des Médailles[131] (Figure 1. 18) in Paris, and has the inscription: ΜΑΕΙΕΗ.

4. There is another similar gem in Rome, in the National Archaeological Museum[132] (Figure 1.19); here the bull's head rests on that of the

---

[130] M. Maaskant-Kleibrink, *Catalogue of the Engraved Gems in the Royal Coin Cabinet, The Hague* (The Hague-Wiesbaden: Government Publ. Office, 1978), 172, no. 1117.

[131] Delatte-Derchain, no. 401.

[132] *SSG* II, Ro 28. C.W. King, *Antique Gems and Rings*, II (2nd edition, London: 1872), plate LIV, 9 and p. 71, no. 9, published an identical gem, but it is described as a red jasper.

Figure 1.17B

boar; on the obverse side the inscription reads: Ῥουφίνα, on the reverse side: ΜΟΙΣΡΩ.

5. A specimen in the British Museum[133] shows Eros, the boar, holding a goat's head and has the inscription: Πριβάτα ΜΟΥΙΣΡΩ.

6. On a red jasper in the Glyptothek in Munich[134] the boar holds a cock; the inscription is: ΤΕΡ.

7. A brown jasper in the Hadrien Rambach collection (Figure 1.20) in London, shows the bull's head in the mouth of the animal, and the inscription: ΜΟΝΝΙ ΣΑΕ ΜΟΥΙΣΡΩ.

---

[133] H.B. Walters, *Catalogue of the Engraved Gems and Cameos: Greek, Etruscan and Roman in the British Museum* (London: British Museum, 1926), no. 1515 (not in Michel's catalogue).
[134] *AGDS* I.3, *München*, no. 2849.

**Figure 1.18A** Yellow jasper in the Cabinet des Médailles, Paris, representing a boar holding a bull's head in its mouth (photograph by the author).

Reprinted with the permission of the Cabinet des Médailles.

8. A green jasper, in the Skoluda collection[135] in Hamburg, shows only a boar or pig swallowing a human figure. The inscription—τὸ τῆς φιλίας—signifies "the (phylactery?) of love."

Furthermore, the image of Eros suggests a use of those amulets for love magic. If this is correct, the names of Ῥουφίνα, "Rufina," and of Πριβάτα, "Privata,"[136] could be those of desired women, the objects of the charm.

The gem representing the emasculated Kronos was placed at the center of Aphrodite's diadem and was supposed to be the most powerful love charm; the boar was depicted on gems of the same kind. The copulating boars were obviously linked to sex and reproduction, whereas the gems with this animal holding the head of another animal in its mouth were probably also connected with sexual and love affairs.

---

[135] Michel, *Die magischen Gemmen*, p. 330, no. 48.2, plate 58.1
[136] For example: *AE* (1962): 394; *AE* (2003): 249; *AE* (1990): 88; Caecin(i)ae Privatae; *CIL* II, 4048: Privat[a] Calpurnia Eutane; *CIL* III, 2236: Aurelia Privata; *CIL* VI, 25059: Pribat(a)e.

**Figure 1.18B** Reverse side.

**Figure 1.19A** Yellow jasper in the National Archaeological Museum, Rome, representing a boar holding a bull's head over its mouth (photograph by the author).

Reprinted with the permission of the National Archaeological Museum.

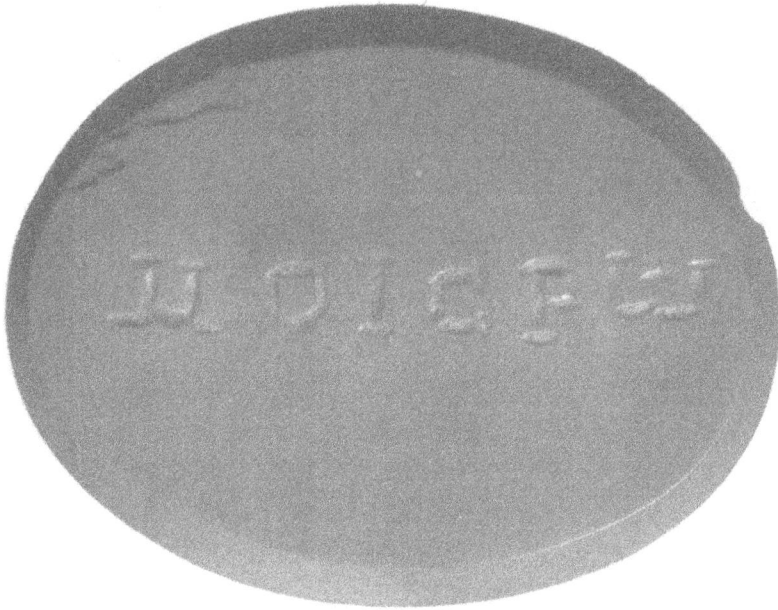

**Figure 1.19B**  Reverse side.

**Figure 1.20**  Brown jasper in the Hadrien Rambach collection, London, representing a boar holding a bull's head in its mouth.

Reprinted with the permission of the Hadrien Rambach collection.

# Chapter 2

# NEW READING OF THE OSIRIS MYTH
# IN NEAR-EASTERN MAGIC

# THE "LITTLE MILL" AND KRONOS'S ORACLES

An obsidian gem, previously bought in Aleppo, Syria, by Henry Seyrig and now at the Cabinet des Médailles in Paris, shows a very peculiar iconography (Figure 2.1). The mummified Osiris is represented on a bed, at whose feet the donkey-headed Seth is standing. There is no doubt that he is Seth, who cut Osiris into pieces, and to whom magicians often resorted so as to threaten Osiris and force him to do things in the realm of the dead.[1] This disquieting image is accompanied by the inscription: χαῖρε Ὄσιρι: "Hail, Osiris!" On the reverse side there are *charakteres* and two magical words: κοδηρε and σαμψουχίθα. The bevel is also inscribed, but the stone is broken in many areas of the border and therefore it is impossible to read clearly.

To understand this iconography it is beneficial to adduce the secret doctrines of Kronos, rather than the Egyptian myth of Osiris. In fact we know that Osiris and Kronos were often linked during the Imperial Age.[2]

**Figure 2.1A**  Obsidian in the Cabinet des Médailles, Paris, representing Seth and Osiris (identified with Kronos) (photograph by the author).

Reproduced with the permission of the Cabinet des Médailles.

---

[1] Cf., e.g., *PGM* VII, 940–68; XII, 141–43; *PDM* XIV, 451–8.

[2] See, e.g., Macrobius. I.7.14–5.

**Figure 2.1B   Reverse side.**

In the great magical papyrus of the Bibliothèque Nationale in Paris[3] we find the following recipe:

> Oracle of Kronos in great demand, called "little mill": Take two measures of salt and grind with a handmill while saying the formula many times until the god appears to you. Do it at night in a place where grass grows. If while you are speaking you hear the heavy step of [someone] and a clatter of iron, the god is coming bound with chains, holding a sickle. But do not be frightened since you are protected by the phylactery that will be revealed to you. Be clothed with clean linen in the garb of a priest of Isis. Offer to the god moss of a tree together with a heart of a cat and horse manure.
>
> *The formula to be spoken while you are mixing is this: Formula:* "I call you, the great, holy, the one who created the whole inhabited world, against whom the transgression was committed by your own son, you whom Helios bound with adamantine fetters lest the universe be mixed together, you hermaphrodite, father of the thunderbolt, you who hold down those under the earth, AIE O PAIDALIS, PHRENOTEICHEIDÔ STYGARDÊS SANKLEON GENECHRONA KOIRAPSAI KÊRIDEU THALAMNIA OCHOTA ANEDEI:

---

[3] *PGM* IV, 3086–124; transl. W.C. Grese (except for the translation of σφάγνος as "moss of a tree," and not "sage").

come, master, god, and tell me by necessity concerning the NN matter, for I am the one who revolted against you, PAIDOLIS MAINOLIS MAINOLIEUS." These are to be said while the salt is being ground.

*And the formula which compels him is:* "KYDOBRIS KODÊRIEUS ANKYRIEUS XANTOMOULIS." You say these things when he appears threateningly, in order that he might be subdued and speak about the things you ask.

*The phylactery in great demand for him [is]:* On the rib of a young pig carve Zeus holding fast the sickle and this name: "CHTHOUMILON." Or let it be the rib of a black, scaly, castrated boar.

*Dismissal:* "ANAEA OCHETA THALAMNIA KÊRIDEU KOIRAPSA GENECHRONA SANÊLON STYGARDÊS CHLEIDÔ PHRAINOLE PAIDOLIS IAEI, go away, master of the world, forefather, go to your own places in order that the universe be maintained. Be gracious to us, lord.

Among the magical words we note "Kêrideu" —Kronos's secret name— which is also known thanks to other sources.[4] Perhaps the *vox* Kodêrieus is related to *kodêre*, which is one of the *voces* of a famous magical *logos* for Persephone. In this *logos* Persephone is identified with Ereschigal (queen of the realm of the dead, wife of Nergal in Mesopotamian mythology) and other goddesses of the night and the netherworld.[5]

The occurrence of Kêrideu and Kodêrieus in the same spell leads us back to Kronos, leaving Osiris aside for a while. The second word on the gem, "Sampsychitha," is formed from the Greek name for marjoram, σάμψουχος (*sàmpsouchos*), which is, in fact, an Egyptian word: "herb of Souchos" (*sm Sbk*).[6] It corresponds to *Majorana hortensis*.[7]

A passage of PGM XIII,[8] copied from the *Eighth book of Moses*, quotes the series of seven incenses of the seven planetary gods:

> Kronos' own incense is styrax because it is heavy and fragrant; the one of Zeus is malabathon, Ares' is kostos, Helios' is incense, the one of Aphrodite is Indian spikenard, Hermes' is cassia and Selene's is myrrh.

It is said that these pieces of information came from Manetho's book and that the *Moses Key* (i.e., a part of the *Eighth book of Moses*) gave further

---

[4] *PGM* IV, 3105, cf. 3119. Cf. A. Mastrocinque, *Studi sul Mitraismo (il Mitraismo e la magia)* (Roma: Giorgio Bretschneider, 1998), 5–6

[5] It is the Yessemigadôn *logos* (e.g., *PGM* II, 35-38: Yessemigadôn Ortho Baubô noêre soire soirê sankanthara Ereschigal sankistê dôdekakistê akrourobore kodêre; V, 423–6).

[6] W. Vycichl, *Dictionnaire étymologique de la langue copte* (Leuven: Peeters, 1983), 189. Plinius, *Naturalis historia* XXI.61 says that the term was used by the Syrians and Egyptians. In Athenaeus XV.18 the so-called "Naucratite wreath" is defined as one made of *sampsouchos*, a flower that was abundant in Egypt.

[7] A.C. Andrews, "Marjoram as a Spice in the Classical Era,"*CPh* 56, (1961): 78, who notes (78 and note 99) that later writers associate this plant with Cyzicus, Cyprus, Syria, and Egypt.

[8] *PGM* XIII, 17–26. Furthermore, the papyrus mentions incenses and flowers of the seven planets. However, the order in which they are mentioned does not correspond to any planetary order that we know. It is possible that the quotation was not very accurate, for the practitioner had to use the seven substances all together. In this case marjoram is quoted in the first place.

information. After that the papyrus continues by saying: "Take the seven flowers of seven stars that are the following: marjoram, white lily, lotus, herephyllinon, narcissus, white pansy and rose." Therefore we have the following series:

| Kronos | Zeus | Ares | Helios | Aphrodite | Hermes | Selene |
|---|---|---|---|---|---|---|
| styrax | malabathron | kostos | incense | spikenard | cassia | myrrh |
| marjoram | white lily | lotus | herephyllinon | narcissus | white pansy | rose |

The planetary order is the canonical one for Imperial times. The same order was also used to assign a single vowel to each planetary god, by shifting the tones from the highest of Selene: E, to arrive at the lowest of Kronos: Ô.[9] The name Sampsouchitha seems to be an adjective that depicts Kronos as the god of marjoram.[10]

Yet, the obverse side of the gem shows Osiris, not Kronos. This Egyptian god lived in a sort of sleep. He was living, but living in the realm of the dead, wrapped in his bandages. The codices of Dioscorides[11] report the Egyptian names of marjoram: γόνος <'Οσ>ίρεως, or ὁμόγονος "Ισεως: "generation of Osiris," "similar generation of Isis." In Imperial times there was a widespread belief that Kronos was sleeping forever in a place where Zeus had confined him as a prisoner. The chains were an iconographical feature proper to this aged god, as we have seen in the "Mill of Kronos" recipe. In addition, the sleeping Kronos was also described in fragments of Orphic works, which have been carefully analyzed by Jan Waszink.[12] Let us examine the most important among them. An extract of an Orphic poem[13] affirms that Kronos, after eating a deceptive food, fell asleep. Another fragment[14] says that Nyx the goddess of night suggested to Zeus

---

[9] Cf. Mastrocinque, *Studi sul Mitraismo*, 8. In the astrological treatises that assign a plant to each planetary god marjoram is never listed; sage or asphodel is assigned to Kronos: A. Delatte, "Le traité des plantes planétaires d'un manuscrit de Léningrad", *Annuaire de l'Inst. de Philol. et d'Hist. Orient. et Slaves* 9, 1949 = ΠΑΓΚΑΡΠΕΙΑ, *Mélanges H. Grégoire* I, (Bruxelles: Secrétariat des Éd. de l'Institut, 1949), 145–77, part. 155–56; cf. also A.J. Festugière, *La révélation d'Hermès Trismégiste. I. L'astrologie et les sciences occultes* (Paris: Lecoffre, 1944), 146–60.

[10] On the Syrian hyssop (*Origanum syriacum sive Majorana syriaca*) and its uses in protective magic in the Near East: R. Hawley, "Hyssop in the Ugaritic Incantation RS 92.2014*," *JANER* 4 (2004): 29–70.

[11] III.41 (III, 39 Wellmann).

[12] J. H. Waszink, "The Dreaming Kronos in the Corpus Hermeticum," *Annuaire de l'Inst. de Philol. et d'Hist. Orient. et Slaves* 9, 1949 = ΠΑΓΚΑΡΠΕΙΑ, *Mélanges H. Grégoire*, II (Bruxelles: Secrétariat des Éd. de l'Institut, 1950): 639–53. On this topic, see A.P. Bos, *Cosmic and Meta-cosmic Theology in Aristotele's Lost Dialogues* (Leiden: Brill, 1989). I have recently dealt with this topic in *Des mystères de Mithra aux mystères de Jésus* (Stuttgart: Steiner, 2009).

[13] A. Bernabé, ed., *Orphicorum et Orphicis similium testimonia et fragmenta. Poetae Epici Graeci.* Pars II.1–3 (Munich/Leipzig: Teubner [II: 1–2], 2004, 2005; Berlin: de Gruyter, 2007 [II:3]), 224.

[14] Bernabé, 187; cf. O. Kern, ed., *Orphicorum fragmenta* (Berlin: Weidmann, 1922), 154; Bernabé, 220, 225.

that he should get Kronos drunk by drinking honey, and therefore Kronos was the first of the living beings to know sleep. In this way Zeus was able to emasculate him.

Other fragments speak of Kronos's revelations. One of those extracts asserts that Nyx was feeding Kronos,[15] and giving advice to Zeus during his work of creation.[16] As claimed by another fragment,[17] Zeus, when he was creating the world, went to consult the oracle of Nyx and also asked for Kronos's help. Another fragment observes that Zeus liberated his father from fetters and was seeking his benevolence; furthermore he got Nyx's oracles, and Kronos gave him helpful directions when he was creating.[18]

Proclos the Neoplatonist describes those fragments (that we have just referred to) in his Commentary on Plato's *Republic, Kratylos,* and *Timaeus.* He gives the following interpretation of those Orphic myths[19]: Zeus was imitating Kronos, and during his sleep he was lifted to the noetic world, that is, to the world of Ideas.[20] He also gained inspiration from the revelations of Kronos when he was accomplishing the creation. In the opinion of Proclos, Kronos transmitted the principles of intelligible truth, that is, of the Platonic Ideas. According to a Hermetic treatise,[21] "the sight of Good does not damage, but fills one with all immortality, and therefore those who can reach a part of this sight, fall asleep, relinquish their body and often reach the most beautiful vision, as it happened to Ouranos and Kronos, our ancestors."

According to Waszink,[22] Kronos unveiled what he saw in his dream by speaking in his sleep. A passage of Plutarch's *de facie in orbe Lunae*[23] suggests such an explanation. This author says that Zeus made Kronos fall asleep; the latter was in a rocky cave, on an island, and birds fed him with ambrosia; gods and humans took care of him and he gave many oracular answers. Indeed his oracles were revelations of his dreams. More precisely,[24] Plutarch maintains that Kronos knew Zeus's thoughts, and, when dreaming, he communicated these thoughts to demons who were

---

[15] Bernabé, 182.

[16] Bernabé, 237.

[17] Bernabé, 237.

[18] Bernabé, 239.

[19] Or he takes it over from other Neoplatonic philosophers.

[20] Procl., *in Tim.* 135, 28 ff.; 138, 15 ff. Kroll.

[21] *Corpus Herm.* X.4-5.

[22] See p. 651.

[23] Plutarchus, *De facie in orbe Lunae* 941 F-942 A. Plutarch affirms that Kronos "sees in a dream Zeus' forethought" (*prodianoeitai*). This passage has been interpreted as if Kronos, thanks to his dreams, suggested to Zeus the fundamental laws of creation, or as if Zeus's forethoughts conditioned the dreams of Kronos; cf. L. Albanese, "Saturno nei misteri di Mithra", *SMSR* 67 (2001): 63-64.

[24] Cf. H. Cherniss, *Plutarch, Moralia,* XII (Cambridge, Mass.: Harvard University Press, 1957), 188; Bos, *Cosmic and Metacosmic,* 77.

surrounding him. Thus the humans could know Zeus's thoughts through the demons.

Tertullian[25] alludes to the Kronos (or Saturnus) dream and claims that Kronos was the first to dream in this world; in addition, Tertullian asks Aristotle to forgive him for laughing at this myth. It is evident that Aristotle dealt with this topic in one of his lost dialogues, maybe in the *Protrepticus*,[26] or in the *De anima sive Eudemus*,[27] which is perhaps to be identified with the *Protrepticus*.[28]

## ORACULAR OSIRIS AND THREATENING SETH

The obsidian gem's iconography could be interpreted as a portrayal of Seth forcing the sleeping Osiris to reveal his oracles. Seth was indeed a threat to Osiris, who was forced to reveal what he was seeing in his dreams. The shift from Kronos to Osiris is proven by the means that were used to force the oracular god to act, according to the "little mill." This recipe of the magical papyrus does indeed describe the constricting spells used to overcome Kronos. It is said that Zeus used violence against Kronos and that Helios put Kronos in chains. The performer of the ritual should say that it was he who revolted against Kronos, therefore he identified himself with Zeus.

Admittedly, the gems could indeed be used in rituals that were supposed to provide the practitioner with prophetic dreams, in which a god,[29] and especially Sarapis,[30] appeared. Sarapis[31] was the Hellenistic form of Osiris and was supposed to give oracles and send dream visions. Moreover Bes, that is, a sort of Osiris as a child, was forced to appear in the night to deliver oracles or do favors.[32]

The gem in the Cabinet des Médailles represents Osiris, but its features recall Kronos. Obsidian was a stone from which amulets of Kronos were carved, and in the first chapter many of these obsidian gems have been taken

---

[25] *De anima* 46.10.

[26] J. H. Waszink, "Traces of Aristotle's Lost Dialogues in Tertullian," *Vig Chr* 1, (1947): 137–49. The reason for the attribution to this work is not strong: Iamblichus, in his *Protrepticus*, spoke of Kronos on the Blessed island; cf. I. Düring, *Aristoteles' Protrepticus. An Attempt of Recontruction* (Stockholm–Göteborg: Almqvist & Wiksell, 1961), Apps. 72 and 168.

[27] Bos, *Cosmic and Meta-cosmic Theology*, chapters I, III, and passim.

[28] A.P. Bos, Aristoteles' "Eudemus" and "Protrepticus": Are They Really Two Different Works, *Dionysius* 8 (1984): 19–51.

[29] R. Wuensch, "Sopra uno scarabeo con iscrizione greca", *BCAR* 27 (1899): 294–9.

[30] *PGM* V, 447–58.

[31] Cf. *SGG* I, no. 60.

[32] Cf. A. Mastrocinque, "Le apparizioni del dio Bes nella tarda antichità. A proposito dell'iscrizione di Gornea", *ZPE* 153 (2005): 243–48.

into account. We have also spoken of the iconography of the Alexandrian Kronos, who was the Greek form of the Egyptian god Souchos, the croco-dile-god of the Fayum. Kronos was holding a little crocodile and a sickle. The adjective *sampsouchitha*, as we have said, comes from the name "herb of Souchos." Additionally, the crocodile could be seen as a symbol of eternity.[33] According to Pseudo-Plutarch's *De fluviis*,[34] Kronos transformed himself into a crocodile to escape from Zeus.

The multiformity of Kronos was a feature that was often highlighted by theologists during Imperial times. Cornutus,[35] the theologist, writes: "the nature of the cosmos—which was precisely called Zeus—became strong and stopped the tranformations of he who moved too much." According to the Vatican Mythographer,[36] Saturnus's head took the forms of a snake, a lion, and a boar, depending on the seasons. In the first chapter we also saw the identification of Kronos with Proteus, the sea god who assumed different shapes to avoid answering questions. He had to be forced to stop his metamorphoses and made to answer.

Christopher Faraone[37] has recently shown that Kronos and the Titans were invoked in magical performances because they were the most ancient living beings in the world—the first ancestors. They were supposed to live in the realm of the dead in a remote land. These features may complete the identification of Kronos with Osiris. One will note that in magical texts of the Imperial Age, Hades is scarcely mentioned. On the gems he is totally absent. In the *defixiones* from Egypt or those that are heavily influenced by Egyptian ideas, Hades is usually replaced by Osiris as the god of the dead.

## OFFERING MOSS, A CAT'S HEART, AND HORSE MANURE

The performer of the "little mill" had to offer Kronos many odd things, according to the magical papyrus. The offering of horse manure seems

---

[33] L. Kàkosy, "Das Krokodil als Symbol der Ewigkeit und der Zeit", *MDAI(K)* 20, (1956): 116 ff. = *Selected Papers (1956–73)*, Studia Aegyptiaca VII (Budapest: Archaeolingua, 1981), 113–8, part. 114.

[34] *De fluviis* 5.3 (where Cleanthes is quoted, the author of a work on the wars of gods).

[35] I.8.

[36] Mythographi Vaticani III (1.8, 155–6 Bode).

[37] "Kronos and the Titans as Powerful Ancestors: A Case Study of the Greek Gods in Later Magical Spells," in *The Gods of Ancient Greece*, eds. J. N Bremmer and A. Erskine (Edinburgh: Edinburgh University Press, 2011) 388–405. Here Faraone writes: "Kronos and the Titans ( . . . ) are invoked in binding spells to restrain or send away anger, and Kronos alone appears in a divination spell that closely recalls contemporary necromantic spells. In what follows, then, I shall show how the defeated Kronos and the Titans evolve quite early on from the 'bad guys' of theogonic poetry to become chthonic agents of anger control and necromancy and how their theogonic prehistory plays into their later roles."

blasphemous. The horse clearly recalls the equine nature of Seth. He was often represented with a donkey's head. By offering such a substance, the performer takes on the behavior of Seth. He was showing contempt for Kronos, who should react as Osiris had done, and submit himself to Seth.[38] Donkey manure or urine was still used in the Middle Ages in Jewish magic to aid childbirth.[39] We know that Seth was the god who opened the womb,[40] and therefore he could favor the delivery. In addition to manure, the performer of the ritual offered salt, moss of a tree, a cat's heart, and was protected by the rib of a pig or a boar.

A recipe in the ninth magical papyrus[41] explains how to prepare an amulet to subdue and to silence; in the invocation to an unknown god the practitioner says: "Bring into subjection . . . for you have put beneath my feet, like my robe, the heart of Sabaoth." The *logos*, which has to be written on the reverse side, is Εὐλαμω σισιρββαιηρ σεσιφερμου Χνουωρ Αβρασαξ.

The heart of a cat could replace a lion's heart, which was extremely difficult to have at one's disposal. One will also notice that the performer offered horse's, not donkey's, manure. Maybe the former was more easily available and totally identical to the latter. Also the offering of moss, instead of wood, or boughs of a tree, had meaning. Maybe it alluded to an old tree. The use of the rib of a pig or a boar shows the existence of two forms of the ritual, or even of two preexisting recipes. The rib of an old, black castrated boar was a proof of the killing of Kronos's animal avatar, whereas the rib of the pig was a less precise allusion.

If we accept these substitutions, we get this series: salt, tree, lion, pig/boar. In the first chapter we took into account the passage of the great magical Papyrus of Paris, where the god is adressed with these words:

> "Hail, Snake and invincible lion, natural
> sources of fire. And hail, clear water and
> lofty-leafed tree!"[42]

In this magical and oracular performance the practitioner acted as if he were Menelaus forcing Proteus to deliver his oracle. The *Odyssey*[43] in

---

[38] With reference to the identification between Sarapis (i.e., the Hellenistic Osiris) and Kronos–Saturnus: Macrobius I.7.14-5; Martianus Capella, *De nuptiis* II.185; about his identification with Zeus, Hades and Helios: Iulian., *Or.* IV.136 A.

[39] P. Schäfer and Sh. Shaked, *Magische Texte aus der kairoer Geniza*, I, Texte und Studien zum Antike und Judentum 42 (Tübingen: Mohr-Siebeck, 1994), 94-5.

[40] A.A. Barb, "Seth or Anubis," *JWCI* 22 (1959), 367-71; cf. R.K. Ritner, "A Uterine Amulet in the Oriental Institute Collection," *JNES* 43 (1984): 209-21.

[41] *PGM* IX, 1-14.

[42] *PGM* IV, 939-41; cf. *PGM* IV, 941 = Homer, *Odyssey* IV.458.

[43] Homer, *Odyssey* IV.418 e 456-8.

fact narrates how Proteus transformed himself into water, fire, a lion, a snake, a panther, a large boar, and a tree. Menelaus attracted Proteus, the Old Man of the Sea, with sealskin. In a similar way the performer of the "little mill" attracted Kronos by means of milled salt, for this god was the lord of seawater.

It is worth mentioning another recipe, which is also reported in the great magical papyrus of Paris.[44] It is that of Nephotes to Psammetichos, king of Egypt. Here the practitioner, wrapped like a corpse, invokes Typhon (i.e., Seth) until a divine sea falcon appears. Thanks to other prayers, the practitioner acquires a divine nature and can begin a request for bowl divination and necromancy and address whatever god or dead man he wants. At the end he dismisses the requested god by pronouncing the most terrible name of Typhon.

Here we find again the magician who is resorting to using Seth to force Osiris, or another god or a dead man, to deliver an oracle or to do something. One should note that all the gods are supposed to obey Seth. The famous curse tablets from Porta San Sebastiano, known as Sethian lamellae, bear texts in which Seth is appealed to and also depicted as a horse-headed god, used to force Osiris, also called Eulamô ("eternity"), to subdue a ghost and make him obey the practitioner.[45]

## HIDDEN AND BLACK

Osiris was also the lord of water, according to Greek theology, and especially Plutarch's *De Iside et Osiride*, chapters 33, 39. This influence over water also appears in Egyptian theology, which supposed that the flooding of the Nile was caused by the sweating mummy of Osiris.[46] The Egyptian god produced fresh water, whereas saltwater was the domain of Seth, the god of sterility.[47] In direct opposition to Seth, Osiris brought fertility. Perhaps this issue of fertility is not an unsurmountable difference between the Greek Kronos and the Egyptian Osiris, which could prevent theologists from identifying them. Both were forcefully removed from their realms and confined to the realm of the dead. Both were hidden. Both were living

---

[44] *PGM* IV, 154–260; transl. N. O'Neil.

[45] See A. Mastrocinque, "Le defixiones di Porta San Sebastiano", *MHNH* 5 (2005): 45–60.

[46] The Shabaka stela mentions this; cf. also J. Vandier, *Le papyrus Jumilhac* (Paris: Centre National de la Recherche Scientifique, 1962), 22; Chaeremon, fr.17 D van der Horst = Eusebius, *Praeparatio Evangelica* III.11. R. Merkelbach and M. Totti, *Abrasax. Ausgewählte Papyri religiösen und magischen Inhalts*, I, Papyrologica Coloniensia 17.1 (Opladen: Westdeutsche Verlag, 1990), 3–10, esp. 7, deal with this recipe of the 4th magical papyrus, and underline the link between the sun god and the Nile water.

[47] Plutarchus, *De Iside et Osiride* 32.

as they slept. Both were threatened by a mighty god: one by Zeus and the other by Seth. Both were supposed to reveal the hidden truth they learned in their dreams. Gems that depicted them were always carved on black, often obsidian, stone.

In case all this proof is insufficient, the existence of a Roman statue might be more persuasive. The statue includes a famous family grouping that is kept in the Vatican museum, and depicts a father as Kronos and a son as Harpokrates, that is, as Osiris's son (Figure 2.2).[48] It is possible that this monument is of funerary character and that the deceased, that is, he to whom the monument is dedicated, namely, Cornutus—is portrayed as Kronos–Saturnus.

Further evidence exists in the form of coins: Several coins of the Tetrarchic period,[49] issued in honor of deceased emperors (*consecratio* issues), show the bust of the deified emperors with their heads covered by the flap of the *toga* (Figure 2.3). The toga was not the clothing of the Pontifex Maximus, for these emperors were deceased and there was already a new Pontifex Maximus. Rather, this was the clothing of Kronos–Saturnus. In Egypt an ancient custom allowed the deceased to be identified with Osiris, and probably Kronos was the god with whom deified men were similarly identified in the Hellenistic and Roman iconographical tradition. The coin of Gallienus in Figure 2.4 proves that Kronos became a god of Aeternity, like Osiris and the divinized emperors.

The gem in the Cabinet des Médailles was previously kept in the collection of Henry Seyrig, who bought it in Aleppo. Therefore, it is probable that the gem was cut in Syria and not in Egypt. Its iconography does not depend on true, sacerdotal Egyptian tradition, but on Hellenistic theology. Sophisticated Near-Eastern speculation used Egyptian iconography to represent Kronos. Also many practitioners of the magical recipes were required to be clothed as Egyptian priests. In the same way Kronos was clothed and featured as Osiris. This Kronos was not, or not only, the Hesiodic god, but was first of all the result of a philosophical and theological refashioning of a Near-Eastern god by Magi or Chaldeans.

---

[48] H. Wrede, *Consecratio in formam deorum* (Mainz am Rhein: 1981), 253–54; no. 160, plate 14; F. Baratte, *LIMC* VIII Supplement no. 19.

[49] See, for example, *RIC* VI, 518, 48 (Maximinianus Herculius); *RIC* VI, 326, 127 (Constantius Chlorus).

**Figure 2.2** Funerary Roman statue representing the deceased as Kronos and his son as Harpokrates (photograph by the author).

Reproduced with the permission of the Vatican Museum.

**Figure 2.3**   Bronze coin created in honor of the deceased and divinized Constantius Chlorus (from Internet auction catalogues).

**Figure 2.4**   Antoninianus of  Gallienus representing Kronos as an image of Aeternitas (from Internet auction catalogues).

# Chapter 3

# HELIOS–SHIVA: PORPHYRY, ARDHANARISVARA, AND A MAGICAL GEM IN NAPLES

# THE PECULIAR HELIOS ON THE HELIOTROPE GEM

A heliotrope gem in the National Archaeological Museum in Naples[1] (Figure 3.1) depicts the god Helios with peculiar features and a series of inscribed magical names. My purpose in this chapter is to show that this god was conceived by a very sophisticated theologist of the 3rd century CE, who was able to merge the Egyptian form of the sun (Harpokrates) with the Indian Brahmanic iconography of an androgynous Shiva. This god is accompanied by a series of symbols and by an animal-headed creator god, who looks to him during his creative activity. The description of the carved figures is as follows: A naked pantheistic god, who may be named Helios, is standing on a prostrate human corpse. He is viewed from the front, the form of his sex is not precisely recognizable; his arms are slightly opened on both sides. His head is surrounded by 12 large rays, between which the word ΧΑΡΧΕΝΔΑΒΡΑΗ can be read. A thin animal skin, its legs hanging down on its right side, covers his chest. With his left hand he is holding a herald staff or caduceus under which an oval object with two points can be seen. The latter could be the bag of Pan, as it is shown in another gem.[2] The god's right hand is holding a strange long scepter, composed of a vegetal staff interrupted in the middle part by two little globes and ending with a branch (palm?) and a compound of globes. Perhaps this is a sort of thyrsos. On the left side of the gem a small animal-headed god is standing and looking up toward Helios. His head could be that of a dog or a wolf. He is ithyphallic, holding a whip and a double axe. On the right side a winged thunderbolt and a snake can be seen.

The Greek inscriptions on this gem read as follows: On the reverse side: ΣΕΜΕΣΕΙΛΑΝΞ ΜΙΧΑΗΛ ΑΧΕΛΩ ΙΟΥ ΙΟΥ ΙΟΥ; on the lower part: ΑΚΙΡΟΚΟΜΑ
On the bevel: [ ca. 6 ] ΩΑΙΑΒΛΑΝΑΘΑΝΑΛΒΡΕΜΩΝΥΨΙΜΕΔΩΗΙΑΩ
[ ca. 4-5 ] ΣΕΣΕΝ[ΒΑΡΦΑΡ]ΑΝΓΗΣΑΡΣΕΝΟΘΗΒΑΚΡΑΜΜΑΧΑΜΑΡΕΙ
ΛΥΒΙΑΙΟΣ ΑΒΡΑ[ . . .

---

[1] U. Pannuti, *Museo Archeologico Nazionale di Napoli. La collezione glittica*, II (Roma: Istituto Poligrafico e Zecca dello Stato, 1994, no. 269; A. Mastrocinque, in *387 a.C. Ambrogio e Agostino. Le sorgenti dell'Europa, Catalogo della mostra* (Milano: Olivares, 2003), 425, no. 266; idem, *Sylloge gemmarum gnosticarum*, II, Na19. The measurements in centimeters are: 1.78 x 1.24 x 0.62, the lower part is damaged. No information about its provenance is known. And I am very grateful to the Soprintendente Maria Luisa Nava and to the keeper of the numismatic department, Dr. Teresa Giove, for having permitted this research in 2005. For a previous approach to the magical gems in Naples cf. A. Mastrocinque, "Studi sulle gemme gnostiche", ZPE 120, 1998, 111–21.
[2] E. Zierlein-Diehl, *Glaspasten im Martin-von-Wagner-Museum der Universität Würzburg*, I (Munich: Prestel, 1986), no. 718.

**Figure 3.1A**   Green jasper stained red in Naples, National Archaeological Museum (photograph by the author).

Reprinted with the permission of the National Archaeological Museum.

**Figure 3.1B** Reverse side.

Figure 3.2    Drawing of a gem that represents, on the reverse, the creator god in front of an important god in the form of an eagle.

Reprinted from J. Macarius and J. Chifflet, *Abraxas seu Apistopistus* (Antwerp: 1657), plate IV, 16.

One can recognize the following known words: Σεμεσιλαμψ (eternal sun),[3] Μιχαὴλ (Michael), αχελ[4] Αβλαναθαναλβ(α) (Ablanathanalba), βρέμων (thundering),[5] ὑψιμέδων (he whose thought is very high), Ἰάω σε(σεν)γενβαρφαρανγης (Iao Sesengenbarpharanges), ἀρσενόθη(λυς) (hermaphrodite), Ακραμμαχαμαρει βίαιος (violent), Αβρα(σαξ?). Ἀρσενόθηλυς signifies "hermaphrodite," and this is a characteristic of some Gnostic divinities, such as Barbelo and Ialdabaoth.

## THE CREATOR GOD

Before beginning our research on the hermaphroditic nature of the god, we should report the results of our previous studies on the animal-headed whipping god.[6] This minor god is the creator. In fact, the same whipping god is portrayed on another gem known only from early modern engravings (see Figure 3.2).[7] It represents the anguipede cock and, on the opposite

---

[3] Cf. M.G. Lancellotti, "Σεμεσ(ε)ιλαμ: una messa a punto", *ZPE* 132,(2000): 248–54. The ending "–lanx" may be a mistake made by the gem cutter.

[4] Cf. perhaps *PGM* VII, 325: αχερω = "spirit king"; or *PGM* LVIII, 33: αχελθε. See P.J. Sijpesteijn, "Zu einigen kölner Gemmen", *ZPE* 51 (1983: 116); on the words αχε and αχεβυκρων: "splendor of light."

[5] Cf. *PGM* V, 471: ὑψιβρεμέτα Ζεῦ.

[6] A. Mastrocinque, "The divinatory kit from Pergamon and Greek magic in late antiquity," *Journal of Roman Archaeology* 15, (2002): 174–87.

[7] J. Macarius and J. Chifflet, *Abraxas seu Apistopistus* (Antwerp: Officina Plantiniana Balthasaris Moreti, 1657), plate IV 16; A. Gorlaeus, *Dactyliotheca*, II (Amsterdam: Henricus à Damme, 1707) no. 345; B. de Montfaucon, *L'antiquité expliquée* (Paris: DeLaulne, 1719–24) = *Antiquity explained* (English trans, London: Garland, 1721), 2, plate 48.

**Figure 3.3**   Drawing of a jasper gem that probably represents the creator god.

Reprinted from A. Capello, *Prodromus iconicus sculptilium gemmarum Basilidiani amulectici atque talismani generis* (Venice: 1702), no. 153.

face, an eagle with a serpent twisted round its legs; in front of them the dog-headed god appears, holding a triangular object in his left hand, and masturbating with the other. There may be another representation of this god (here, Figure 3.3) on the jasper published in the XVIII century.[8] The identity of this god is revealed by a lapis lazuli gem (Figure 3.4) once in the Library of S. Geneviève in Paris, and later in the Southesk collection.[9]

---

[8] A. Capello, *Prodromus iconicus sculptilium gemmarum Basilidiani amulectici atque talismani generis* (Venice: typis Hieronymi Albriccij, 1702; reprint with introduction by M. Gabriele, A. Mastrocinque, and F. Barbierato, Udine: Forum, 2008), no. 153, and reproduced by P. Zazoff, *AGDS* III, *Braunschweig, Göttingen, Kassel* (Wiesbaden: 1970), no. 129, who describes the small figure above the anguipede cock as a baboon. A similar masturbating god appears on another gem in Paris: A. Delatte and Ph. Derchain, *Les intailles magiques gréco-égyptiennes* (Paris: Bibliothèque Nationale, 1964) no. 227 (though according to the authors he has a donkey's head).

[9] Cl. du Molinet, *Cabinet de la bibliothèque de Ste Geneviève* (Paris: A. Dezallier, 1692), plate 30, I–II; B. de Montfaucon, *Antiquity explained*, II, plate 53; ed. H. Carnegie, *Catalogue of the Collection of Ancient Gems Formed by J., Ninth Earl of Southesk, K.T.* (London: Quaritch, 1908), 1 no. N 24; *SGG* I, 290. Ph. Derchain, "Le démiurge et la balance", in *Religions en Égypte hellénistique et romaine. Colloque Strasbourg 1967* (Paris: Presses Universitaires de France, 1969), 32 and plate I.3, explains why the balance as a symbol of the pantheistic magical god signified the masturbating act of Atum (Egyptian *iwśw*, "[masturbating] hand," was pronounced like *iwsw*, "balance"). J.-F. Quack, "The so-called Pantheos. On Polymorphic Deities in Late Egyptian Religion," *Aegyptus et Pannonia* 3 (2006): 184–85, argued that Derchain's interpretation is false because the gems that depict the god with a scale at the top of the penis are modern. A direct study of several of those gems allows me to ascertain that they are ancient.

71

**Figure 3.4**   Lapis lazuli gem once in the Southesk collection.

Reprinted from H. Carnegie, ed., *Catalogue of the Collection of Ancient Gems Formed by J., Ninth Earl of Southesk, K.T.* (London: 1908), 1, no. N 24.

Here the seven planetary gods are depicted in a mixed Graeco-Egyptian form, and Jupiter has the guise of Re-Atum, the Egyptian creator god identified with the Sun, holding a whip while masturbating.[10]

The creator god's animal form is often described in the Gnostic treatises.[11] He has a lion's head and his name is Ialdabaoth. In the magical papyri there is an invocation,[12] spoken in the name of Adam, to the god who illuminates the world, who copulates in the ocean, called Kmeph, Helios, the infant god, that is, Harpokrates—creator of justice and dispenser of truth. In the case of the gem in Naples the creator god does not correspond to the solar god, but he is inferior to him. On the other hand, the major god, bearing twelve rays over his head, is a form of the sun and is virtually equal to Harpokrates, the young solar god of Egyptian theology, who was the most popular form of the ancient god Horus. In fact we

---

[10] The obverse of a red-green jasper in the Ägyptisches Museum in Berlin (Philipp, *Mira et magica*, no. 138) shows a radiating lion-headed god accompanied by the names of the Jewish Archangels; the reverse shows the triple Hekate with torches, knives, and whips; in front of her is a god, with the head of a wolf or a dog, holding a whip and a crown in his hands.

[11] Nag Hammadi, "Treatise without title" (also known as Origin of the world) 100, 114, 119; *Hypostasis of the Archons* 94; *Apocryphon of John* BG 37; *Pistis Sophia*, 1.31–32, 39; Origen, *Contra Cels.* VI.30; A. Böhlig and P. Labib, *Die koptisch-gnostische Schrift ohne Titel aus Codex II von Nag Hammadi* (Berlin: Akademie Verlag, 1962), comm. to § 114; G.A.G. Stroumsa, *Another Seed: Studies in Gnostic Mythology* (Leiden: Brill, 1984), 52.

[12] PGM III, 140–57; cf. also *PGM* IV, 1642–3; XXXVIII ver. 15–17.

**Figure 3.5**  Green jasper stained red in the British Museum, London, representing Harpokrates and a snake.

Reproduced by courtesy of the Trustees of the British Museum.

know another gem[13] (Figure 3.5) in the same style and produced by the same workshop, on which Harpokrates is represented with a snake, and this snake has the same form as the snake on the Naples gem.

## THE SUN GOD

The corpse, on which the god is standing, is a common feature in the iconography on magical gems, and it is meant to show the triumph over death or the victory over unjust men.[14] The gem is damaged on the lower side and it is impossible to know the form taken by the corpse's head. The god has the symbols of Helios (the rays), of Hermes (the herald's staff), perhaps of Pan (the bag?), Dionysos (the thyrsos? the animal's skin?), and Heracles (the animal's skin?). He is therefore a pantheistic divinity. In late antiquity Dionysos was identified with the Sun god.[15] In the aretalogy on a third-century inscription from Chalcis[16] Harpokrates

---

[13] Michel, *British Museum*, no. 107. On the reverse side one can read the name of Iaô.

[14] This is the specific case of Nemesis.

[15] Macrobius I.18.12–15; 23.22; cf. Iulianus, *Oratio* IV.148 A ff., *Oratio* VIII (V), 179 B, Proclus, *In Timaeum* 1.446; II.80 and 179.

[16] R. Harder, "Karpokrates von Chalkis und die memphitische Isispropaganda", *Abhandlungen der preussischen Akademie del Wissenschaften* (Berlin: de Gruyter, 1943); Ph. Matthey, "Retour sur l'hymne "arétalogique" de Karpocrate à Chalcis", *Archiv für Religionsgeschichte,* 9 (2007): 191–222.

is identified with Helios, Apollo, Dionysos and is recognized as the higher god, lord of the cosmos. Compound divinities with solar features are known from the age of the late Roman republic.[17] They were conceived to represent a lord of the cosmos, a god who was mightier than the other gods. Usually, compound divine features were given to the divinities of destiny, such as Tyche, or to the hypercosmic Sun, which is depicted in the *Hymn to King Helios* by Julian the Apostate. The theme of the snake occurs in many religious traditions of the Roman period and accompanies the birth of Harpokrates, as we have seen, and of Mithra. Furthermore, the thunderbolt is such a common symbol that one can obtain no precise information about the nature of the god from it.

The most important feature of this god is the hermaphroditism. The inscription says that he is a hermaphrodite (*arsenothelys*) and his image shows an incomplete male sexual apparatus, the large flanks and slim waist of a woman. His left breast is prominent. The most important and mighty divinities of late antiquity were thought to be hermaphrodites,[18] for they were complete in their perfect unity. In several theological systems two almighty gods were conceived: one young and one elder,[19] and they could be hermaphrodites or have no sex at all. This was the case of Kronos, who was thought to be an emasculated god, was prayed to as the hermaphrodite god, and names of male and female divinities were used to adjure him.[20] During the Imperial Age, the theme of divine hermaphroditism was developed in Egyptian and Gnostic theologies.[21] Dionysos was said to be a hermaphrodite.[22] The disguise of Herakles as a woman is typical of the Omphale myth, and was also present in Roman rituality,[23]

[17] M.H. Crawford, *Roman Republican Coinage* (Cambridge: Cambridge University Press, 1974), no. 494/5; cf. G.H. Halsberghe, *The Cult of Sol Invictus* (Leiden: Brill, 1972), 29; L. Musso, "*Eikon tou kosmou* a Merida: ricerca iconografica per la restituzione del modello compositivo", *RIASA* 3rd ser. 6–7 (1983–84): 158.

[18] On divine androgyny in Imperial Age speculations, see L. Brisson, *Le sexe incertain. Androgynie et hermaphroditisme dans l'antiquité* (Paris: Les Belles Lettres, 1994).

[19] For the heretical Jews: A.F. Segal, *Two Powers in Heaven. Early Rabbinic Reports about Christianity and Gnosticism*, Studies in Judaism in Late Antiquity 25 (Leiden: Brill, 1977).

[20] See the first chapter. Cf. PGM IV, 3102: ἀρσενόθηλυ, βροντοκεραυνοπάτωρ; *Kyranides* I, 10, 63–65, ed. Kaimakis.

[21] J. Zandee, "Der Androgyne Gott in Ägypten. Ein Erscheinungsbild des Weltschöpfers", in *Religion im Erbe Ägyptens. Beiträge zur spätantiken Religionsgeschichte zu Ehren von Alexander Böhlig*, ed. M. Görg (Wiesbaden: Harrassowitz, 1988), 240–78; cf. also J.-P. Mahé, *Hermès en Haute-Egypte*, I (Québec: Presses de l'Université Laval, 1978), 36.

[22] Aeschylus, *TGF* III, fr. 61; Euripides, *Bacchae* 353: *thelymorphos*, "having a female aspect"; Theodoretus, *Graecarum affectionum curatio* III.80: Dionysos *gynnis*: "like a woman"; Polyaenus IV.1.1 and M.B. Hatzopoulos, *Cultes et rites de passage en Macédoine* (Athens: 1994), 67, 73–85: Dionysos *pseudanor*: "false man"; Scholium in Lucianum, *De Dea Syria* 28, 187 Rabe: Dionysos *kinaidos*: "catamite"; Lydus, *de mensibus* IV.160: *arsenothelys*: "hermaphrodite"; Hesychius, *Lexikon*, s.v. *Dyalos*: Dionysos *dyalos*: "hybrid"; see also Zacharie le Scholastique, *Vie de Sévère*, ed. M.-A.Kugener, PO 2/1 (Paris: 1903), 34.

[23]Cf. M.Verzar Bass, "L'ara di Lucius Munius a Rieti", *MEFRA* 97 (1985): 295–323.

as it was known then even in late antiquity.[24] According to theological speculations of Imperial times, his twelve labors were symbolized by the twelve zodiacal signs[25] and he was identified with the sun and with time.[26] The twelve letters of ΧΑΡΧΕΝΔΑΒΡΑΗ and the twelve rays of the god could refer to the months or the zodiacal signs.

According to the *Apocryphon of John*,[27] the first son or daughter of the supreme god was the bisexual Barbelo; according to the *Origin of the World*[28] and perhaps the *Nature of the Archons*,[29] the Archons too were bisexual as was their father, the young god Ialdabaoth, and they had both a masculine and a feminine name. In Gnostic theology, sex and separation between male and female genders were among the later steps in the process of creation, whereas paganism kept separate the genders of important cosmic gods, such as Venus and Mars. The theologists who inspired the engraved gem, and who spoke of a god copulating in the ocean,[30] placed the creator god in a higher place in the pantheon hierarchy and gave him a masculine character. The same can be said of the Egyptian myth of Atum. In the Imperial Age an ancient Egyptian pantheistic god was often represented as the creator, who had many animal, vegetal, and human features. He was ithyphallic and all the forms in the world derived from his forms; he was the first father.[31]

---

[24] Lydus, *de mensibus* IV.67.

[25] Eusebius, *Praeparatio evangelica* III.11.25; cf. also 13.17; Eusebius was using a passage of Porphyry: fr. 359 Smith.

[26] Lydus, *de mensibus* IV.46 (= 67 W.); Tzetzes, *Chiliades* II.324; on Cerberos and time: Macrob. I.20.13; cf. O. Gruppe, *RE* Suppl. III (1918): c.1104.

[27] 5, Synopsis 11–12 (*Coptic Gnostic Library*, II.1, 33–34).

[28] 100–102 (*Coptic Gnostic Library*, II.5, 37).

[29] 87 (*Coptic Gnostic Library*, II.4, 237); the text is corrupted: "the rulers . . . body . . . they have . . . female . . . is . . . with the face of a beast."

[30] According to the magical papyri.

[31] R. Merkelbach, *Astrologie, Mechanik, Alchimie und Magie im griechsch-römischen Ägypten*, in *Begegnung von Heidentum und Christentum im spätantiken Ägypten*, Riggisberger Berichte 1 (1993): 49–62; and also Ph. Derchain, "*Le démiurge et la balance*", in *Religions en Égypte hellénistique et romaine* (Paris: Presses Universitaires de France, 1969), 31–34; M. Philonenko, "*Le livre des secrets d'Hénoch*" ibid., 109–16, and, on the side of Egyptology, J. Assmann, "Primat und Traszendenz. Struktur und Genese der ägyptischen Vorstellung eines höchsten Wesens", in *Aspekte der spätägyptischen Religion*, ed. W. Westendorf, Göttinger Orientforschungen IV.9 (Wiesbaden: Harrassowitz, 1979), 7–42; cf. idem, *Re und Amun. Die Krise des polytheistischen Weltbildes in Ägypten der 18.–20. Dynastie*, Orbis Biblicus et Orientalis 51 (Fribourg-Göttingen: Universitaetsverlag & Vandenhoeck und Ruprecht, 1983); idem, *Monotheismus und Kosmotheismus. Ägyptische Formen eines Denkens des Eines und ihre europäische Rezeptionsgeschichte*, Sitzungsberichte der Heidelberger Akademie der Wissenschaften, Philos.-Hist. Klasse 1993, 2nd part Heidelberg: Winter, 1993); idem, *The Search for God in Ancient Egypt* (Ithaca-London: Cornell University Press, 2001), § 9.3; O. Kaper, *The Egyptian God Tutu. A Study of the Sphinx-God and Master of Demons with a Corpus of Monuments*, OLA 119 (Leuven-Paris-Dudley: Peeters, 2003), 91–104; E. Hornung, *Conceptions of God in Ancient Egypt: The One and the Many* (Ithaca-London: Cornell University Press, 1982), 127; J.-F. Quack, "The so-called Pantheos. On Polymorphic Deities in Late Egyptian Religion," *Aegyptus et Pannonia* 3, (2006):175–76.

Many Gnostic works discuss the problem of the gender of the supreme gods, but now is not the time to deal with it. Suffice to say that this is an important feature of several theological streams of the Roman empire.

## CREATION AND THE CONTEMPLATION OF THE PERFECT GOD

Plato[32] said that love produces emissions of a generative substance (semen) thanks to the vision of Beauty, and he interpreted the name of Ouranos as "contemplation of the higher world" (*horôsa ta anô*).[33] The emperor Julian[34] said that "For when the generative substance which is visible in our world desires to beget in the Beautiful and to bring forth offspring, it is further necessary that it should be guided by the substance that, in the region of intelligible beauty, does this very thing eternally and always." Proclus[35] maintains that Kronos could have the beatifying vision described by Socrates. The 10th treatise of the *Corpus Hermeticum* says:

> the vision of the Good ... not only does come more swiftly down to us, but it does us no harm, and is instinct with all immortal life. They who are able to obtain more of this Sight, often fall asleep and from out of the body see the fairest of Visions, just like it happened to Ouranus and Kronos, our ancestors.[36]

As we saw in the second chapter, Waszink[37] focused on a series of Orphic fragments, from which it is possible for us to understand that during Zeus's creative activity, Kronos, kept in a cave and asleep, had many dreams and visions of the metaphysical hyperouranic realms. Therefore Zeus could obtain higher directions so as to create the world correctly.[38] These fragments are sometimes obscure, among other things, they merge Orphic and Neoplatonic ideas. Proclos interpreted[39] this Orphic

---

[32] Plato, *Symposium* 206 A–207 A.

[33] Plato, *Cratylus* 396 B.

[34] *In Helium regem* 24 = 145 A, trans. Wilmer Cave Wright.

[35] *In Cratylum* 162.

[36] *Corpus Hermeticum* X.4–5.

[37] J. H. Waszink, "The Dreaming Kronos in the Corpus Hermeticum," *Annuaire de l'Inst. de Philol. et d'Hist. Orient. et Slaves* 9, 1949 = ΠΑΓΚΑΡΠΕΙΑ, *Mélanges H. Grégoire*, II (Bruxelles: Secrétariat des Éd. de l'Institut, 1950): 639–53, esp. 644–7; cf. J. H. Waszink, "Traces of Aristotle's Lost Dialogues in Tertullian," *Vig. Chr.* 1 (1947): 137–49; L. Albanese, "Saturno nei misteri di Mithra," *SMSR* 67 (2001): 60; and, above all, A.P. Bos, *Cosmic and Meta-cosmic Theology in Aristotle's Lost Dialogues* (Leiden: Brill, 1989).

[38] Fr. 129 Kern = 182 Bernabé; 148 Kern = 224 Bernabé; 154 Kern = 187, 220, 222 et 225 Bernabé (= Porphyrius *de antro nympharum* 16); 155 Kern = 239 Bernabé; 164 Kern = 237 Bernabé. These fragments are quite obscure and their interpretation is very difficult.

[39] Or he uses works of other Neoplatonic thinkers.

tradition and maintained that Zeus imitated Kronos, and during his sleep was elevated to the world of Ideas.[40]

In the context of Gnostic traditions, as they are described by Ireneus, Hippolytus, and Epiphanius, and according to the Gnostic Nag Hammadi library, we learn that these supposed "heretics" conceived the supreme god's first manifestation in human form, the Anthropos.[41] According to Gnostic ideas,[42] women who thought of their lovers during sexual intercourse with their husbands would conceive children similar to the lovers. Pagan thinkers were of the same opinion.[43] Some Gnostic theologists maintained that the divine Wisdom—called Achamot—created while contemplating the Savior's angels.[44] Valentinus said that the divine Mother produced Jesus by thinking of the most sublime things.[45] The devotees of Barbelo said that Ialdabaoth contemplated the material substance and created Nous, a snake-like divine being, and then he listened to his mother's voice and created Man.[46] According to other traditions, the Archons once saw a bright image in the sky and created Man;[47] and again, Divine Providence (Pronoia) saw the perfect angel in the sky, the heavenly Adam, and let flow toward the earth a few rays of her own light, from which Adam was born;[48] or, according to other authors, Adam was born from the fallen semen of Archons.[49] The doctrine of the Peratae speculated a lot about contemplation and generation through the body's different organs.[50]

One can stop here with the topic of contemplation and creation or generation in different religious streams of the Roman Empire, because it is clear enough that the creator god took inspiration from the contemplation of the supreme god, or from the supreme and unified manifestation

---

[40] Tertullianus, *De anima* 46.10 says that perhaps Aristotle dealt with the dreaming Saturnus (i.e., Kronos), in his *Protrepticus* (Waszink, "Traces of Aristotle's Lost Dialogues in Tertullian"), or rather in the *de anima sive Eudemus* [A.P. Bos, "Aristoteles' 'Eudemus' and 'Protrepticus': Are they really two different Works?" in *Dionysius* 8 (1984): 19-51]. See also the recipe of the magical papyri for obtaining prophecies from Kronos: *PGM* IV, 3086–124.

[41] G. Quispel, "Der gnostische Anthropos und die Judische Tradition", *Eranos Jahrbuch* 22 (1953): 195–234, reprinted in *Gnostic Studies*, I (Istanbul: Nederlands Historisch-Archaeologisch Instituut in het Nabije Oosten, 1974).

[42] *Gospel of Philip* 78.

[43] Heliodorus, *Ethiopicae* IV.8.

[44] Irenaeus, *adversus haereses* I.4.5 and 5.6.

[45] Irenaeus, *adversus haereses* I.11.1.

[46] Irenaeus, *adversus haereses* I.30.5–6.

[47] Irenaeus, *adversus haereses* I.24.17.

[48] *Origin of the World* 108, 113, and 115 (*Coptic Gnostic Library*, II.2, 52–3, 61–2, and 65).

[49] *Origin of the World* 114 (*Coptic Gnostic Library*, II.2, p. 63).

[50] Hippolytus, *Refutatio haeresium* V.17.11-12; cf. F. Michelini Tocci, "La cosmogonia dei Perati e il gregge di Giacobbe (e Dante)" in *Omaggio a Piero Treves*, ed. A. Mastrocinque (Padova: Antenore, 1983) 249–60. For other passages on the same theme of contemplation and generation, see Iren., *adv. haer.* I.2, 3; 29.4; *Nature of the Archontes* 94 and 99; Pseudo-Clemens, *Homilia* VIII.18.2.

**Figure 3.6** Limonite gem in the Cabinet des Médailles, Paris, representing the Egyptian polymorphic god (Delatte-Derchain, no. 170) (photograph by the author).

Reprinted with the permission of the Cabinet des Médailles.

of God. This manifestation often had a human form, it was the Anthropos, a sort of Platonic ideal of Man,[51] the perfect man, in which male and female were unified. On the other hand, the Egyptian polymorphic creator god (an example is shown in Figure 3.6) did not contemplate, but engendered from himself the beings, which reproduced the forms of himself.

Gnostic thought also conceived a statue representing the Anthropos. The Naassenes referred to Chaldean doctrines, according to which the

---

[51] Plato, *Respublica* V1.506 D-508 C first said that the supreme god, the Good, manifested himself in the sun. It is perhaps worth mentioning a passage of Epiphanius, *Panarion* XXVI.3.1 (I, 278, ed. Karl Holl), which reports that the *Gospel of Eve* described a vision in which a tall heavenly figure, accompanied by another person of small stature, appeared. A link between these two figures and those on the Naples gem is possible, although completely hypothetical.

Anthropos, or Adam, was begotten forth by the Earth. He was inanimate like a statue, and represented an image of the divine being, who is above, who was celebrated as Adamas.[52]

## INDIAN SHIVAITE INFLUENCES
## ON NEOPLATONIC THEOLOGY

When I first saw the gem in Naples, I had the impression that the style of Helios's image was not Greek, but rather Indian. The movement of his hip, the frontality, and the sensual rendering of the body recalled Indian statuary. My impression was, in fact, correct. In a fragment of Porphyry, from his treatise on Styges's water, we read:

> The Indians[53] who lived in Syria under the reign of the Emesene Antonine[54] had a discussion with the Mesopotamian Bardisanes, and related, as Bardisanes wrote, the following things . . .
>
> They also said that there is a natural big cave, in a big mountain, almost in the middle of the Earth. In this cave there is a statue whose height was estimated to be twelve cubiti. It is standing, with opened arms,[55] in the form of a cross. The right part of his face is masculine and the left feminine. Moreover, in the same way, the right arm and foot and all this half of the body is masculine while the left part is feminine. One is astonished, therefore, when this mix is seen and one could ask how it is possible to see this diversity of the two parts in one body. It is said that on that statue the sun is carved around the right breast, and the moon around the left, and on the arms . . . .[56] In an artistic fashion a number of angels and whatever it is that exists in this world are sculpted, namely the sky, mountains, seas, rivers, oceans, plants, animals and, in short, all the existing things. It is said that God gave this statue to the Son when this latter was creating the world for he had to see a model (in order to create it).[57]

The tale of the Brahmans, led by Sandales, continues by describing other features of this statue and of the cave. The account was found by Porphyry in the book on India by Bardesanes. The most important thing is that Greek and Syrian theologians knew the form of the Indian androgynous god, after which creation was made. We now have the archaeological

---

[52] Hippolytus, *Refutatio haeresium* V.7.5-6.
[53] From other passages it becomes clear that they were Brahmans.
[54] Heliogabalus.
[55] Or hands: *cheiras*: cf. Porfirio, *Sullo Stige*, ed. C. Castelletti (Milan: Bompiani, 2006), 255.
[56] The text is interrupted.
[57] Fr. 7 Smith = fr. 7 Castelletti = Stobaeus I.3.56 (I, 66–70, ed. Curt Wachsmuth).

evidence of the Brahmanic teaching of and merging of Indian and Greek ideas about creation. The gem in the Archaeological Museum in Naples is sound evidence of theological speculation by wise men of the Eastern provinces of the Roman Empire, which takes into account Indian religious ideas. This fact suggests an origination date for the gem in the 3rd century CE, the century of Bardesanes and Porphyry. It was the period of Heliogabalus, the emperor who identified himself with the solar god of Hemesa and sometimes appeared in female disguise.[58]

The statue described by the Brahmans to Bardesanes corresponds to Indian statues of an androgynous form of Shiva, Ardhanarisvara. Excellent investigations on Indian models of Bardesanes and Porphyry's description have recently been made by Joachim Lacrosse[59] and Cristiano Castelletti,[60] although the identification of the model with Ardhanarisvara was first proposed by von Schlegel[61] and accepted by many scholars. Ardhanarisvara means *ardha nārī iśvara*: "Lord half woman"[62] and represents an iconographic and theological development of Shiva joined to his Shakti (that is, his female counterpart), Pārvatī.[63] The couple expresses divine unity and the generative force. The first evidence of this iconography dates back to the 2nd century C.E. and the first sculpture of Ardhanarisvara dates from the end of the 2nd century.[64] Images of this god (Figure 3.7) were very popular and nowadays they are among the preferred forms of Shiva. They are often abundant in symbols, which characterize the male and the female parts. Two statues are especially interesting and clear in depicting these symbols, one stone relief from Abaneri (Gujara – Pratibara),

---

[58] Cf. a recent book by S. Gualerzi, *Né uomo né donna, né dio, né dea. Ruolo sessuale e ruolo religioso dell'imperatore Elagabalo*, (Bologna: Pàtron, 2005).

[59] J. Lacrosse, "Un passage de Porphyre relatif au Shiva androgyne chez les brahmanes d'Inde", *Rev. Philos. Anc.* 20 (2002): 37–56.

[60] Porfirio, *Sullo Stige*, 254–55.

[61] A.W. von Schlegel, *Indische Bibliothek*, II (Bonn: Weber, 1827), 462; cf. also Ch. Lassen, *Indische Alterthumskunde*, III (Leipzig-London: Kittler, 1858), 348–53; J. Fergusson, *History of Indian and Eastern Architecture*, I (London: Murray, 1910), 42; N.J. Banerjea, *The Development of Hindy Iconography* (Calcutta: Kessinger Publishing, 1956), 89; H.W. Haussig, ed., *Wörterbuch der Mythologie*, V. *Götter und Mythen des indischen Subkontinents* (Stuttgart: Klett-Cotta, 1984), s.v. *Zweigottheiten*, 203; H. Boll, "Studien zum griechischen Roman", *Philologus* 66 (Leipzig: Dieterich, 1907): 12–13.

[62] *Iśvara* is Shiva, and *nārī* is Pārvatī.

[63] On Ardhanarisvara cf. the important monography by N. Yadav, *Ardhanarisvara in Art and Literature* (New Delhi: D. K. Printworld, 2001); see also: E. Goldberg, *The Lord Who is Half Woman: Ardhanarisvara in Indian and Feminist Perspective* (Albany: State University of New York Press, 2002).

[64] Yadav, 33. The image of this god on one gold coin of Kanishka III (ca. 240 CE) has been recognized: O.P. Singh, "Ardhanarisvara on the coin of Kaniska," *Journal of the Numismatic Society of India* 30 (1968): 195–8; Yadav, 13 and 35; but other authors prefer to recognize there the normal image of Shiva: P. Srivastava, *Aspects of Ancient Indian Numismatics* (Delhi: Agam Kala Prakashan, 1996), 103–4. An image of this coin is available in R.B. Whitehead, *Catalogue of the Indo-Greek Coins in the Punjab Museum, Lahore*, I *Indo-Greek Coins* (Oxford: Clarendon Press, 1914), 211, plate XIX, 231.

**Figure 3.7**  Granite statue of Shiva Ardhanarishvara, XIV century CE, from the State of Tamil Nadu; Chicago, the Art Institute of Chicago.

Reproduced with permission of the The Art Institute of Chicago. Photography © The Art Institute of Chicago.

from the 9th century, in the collection of the Maharaja of Jaipur,[65] and a bronze statue from the 11th century from Tiruvankadu housed in the Madras Museum.[66] Reliefs of Ardhanarisvara are also cut in caves, for example, on the Elephanta (Bombay) island (5th to 8th centuries) and in Mogalarajapuram (near Vijayawada, in the Andhra Pradesh region), where a statue from the 5th century is kept.[67] Here the god is surrounded by divine beings and symbols of everything to show that he is the origin of every generation.[68] Ardhanarisvara's images show him with a lot of gender features on the left and on the right sides of his/her body, as described by Porphyry. The left female half wears bracelets and ankle rings, bracelets on hands and feet, and is holding a mirror or a lotus stem. The male half is holding a weapon in the form of a trident with ondulate prongs, the *trisûla*; he wears a tiger skin and is adorned by a skull or a snake.[69]

The iconography of the Indian hermaphroditic god is repeated in this small theological treatise carved on the gem. The snake and the animal's skin, maybe the lotus stem too, are also present on the intaglio; the trident has been transformed into the caduceus of the herald god. Other symbols, missing in the Indian models, have been added: the corpse, the thunderbolt, the bag of Pan, and, above all, the animal-headed creator god. This god does not occur in the Indian Ardhanarisvara's iconography, but occurs in the Brahmans' interview with Bardesanes. In Indian art it appears that Shakti is embraced by Shiva and is looking up to him; this attitude symbolized the beginning of creation.[70] But we will also see that the creator was present in Indian literature of the Imperial Age.

The idea of creating as copying after a model is a Platonic one. According to Platonism, everything on the Earth is an imitation of a divine and perfect model. Indian theology gives to Ardhanarisvara or to the couple Shiva–Pārvatī the function of creating. Nevertheless it is true that several images of Ardhanarisvara represent him accompanied by a number of symbols and deities that symbolize the cosmic reality. The idea of condensing everything in the divine unity is a feature of demiurgical gods in several theological systems of the Imperial Age. The Egyptian Pantheos—or polymorphic Bes—is one divinity of this kind.

The doctrines alluded to in Bardesanes and Porphyry recur in the *Upanishads*, that is, in Indian treatises that were known in Imperial times, and not only in India. According to the *Upanishads*, the divine unity is

---

[65] C. Sivaramamurti, *The Art of India* (New York: Abrams, 1974), fig. 61.

[66] Sivaramamurti, fig. 68.

[67] Lacrosse, "Un passage", 44.

[68] Sivaramamurti, 474. Cave 15.

[69] See Yadav, 22–30.

[70] Goldberg, chapter 5.

the Brahman, which is present everywere in the world as well as in the human soul. According to the *Śvetāśvara Upanishad*, Brahman cannot be viewed as a cause. For this reason, Brahman, when acting in this world, manifests itself as Brahman Iśvara, the Lord, the principle of creation. Iśvara is therefore the creator. Iśvara is Brahman who has a form and creates every form. Brahman is formless; Iśvara has a form and could establish a relation between Brahman and the world. The *Upanishads* know one specific creator-god, called Brahma or Hiranya-garbha, which is the World-Soul. He is not clearly distinguished from Iśvara. Brahman, Iśvara, and Hiranya-garbha are the foundations of the manifested world.[71] The *Maitrī-Upanishad* maintains that Brahman has two aspects, the formless and the formed. The formed is caused by the formless. Brahman is light and that which is light is sun (*Maitrī—Upanishad* VI.3). Therefore the Brahmanic doctrines spoken of in Bardesanes were rooted in the theology of the *Upanishads*.

Very few Indian theological treatises were translated into Greek or Latin or summarized and consequently were relatively unknown in the Roman Empire. During the same period when Bardesanes met the Brahmans, the Christian writer Hippolytos reported in his heresiological work several Brahmanic doctrines[72] that correspond to the theology of Sanskrit sources and above all the *Maitrī-Upanishad*.[73] The knowledge of the contents of the *Maitrī-Upanishad* appears to have been quite correct, even though one cannot decide whether the Christian heretics had read a translation or had learned the *Upanishad's* philosophy directly from the Brahmans.

Now we meet again, on the gem, a doctrine of the *Upanishads*, and again this concept appears in the *Maitrī-Upanishad*: the doctrine of Iśvara, or, more precisely, of Ardhanarisvara. One could suppose that Iśvara's theology and Ardhanarisvara's iconography were influenced by Western theologies, and more important, by Platonism, and that the Brahmans— traveling, living, or dwelling for some time in Syria—were the medium between India and Western thought.[74] But there are strong reasons to suppose this influence came in an inverse way, from India to the Hellenistic

---

[71] See S. Radhakrishnan, *The Principal Upanisads* (New York: Allen & Unwin; Harper Collins India, 1969); for a comparison with Plotinus's thought see L.J. Hatab, "Plotinus and the *Upanisads*," in *Neoplatonism and Indian Thought*, ed. R. Baine Harris (Norfolk, VA: International Society for Neoplatonic Studies, 1982), 27–43; A. Magris, "Plotino e l'India", *Annuario Filosofico* 6 (1990), 105–62.

[72] *Refutatio haeresium* I.24.

[73] See J. Filliozat, "La doctrine des Brahmanes d'après saint Hippolyte", *RHR* 130 (1945): 59–91; J.M.F. van Reeth, "Entre Rome, Babylone et les Indes. Bardésane, stoïcien universaliste", *Res Antiquae* 7, 2010, 241–52.

[74] Porphyrius, *De abstinentia* IV.17.10, reports another passage of Bardesanes, who spoke of a Brahman embassy sent to meet the emperor.

world. This is not the place to discuss such a complex topic at length. For us it is enough to have discovered important new evidence of the influence of the *Maitrī-Upanishad* theology on Western theological thought.

After having focused on the debt from the *Upanishads* of the doctrine in Bardesanes and the gem's iconography, it is difficult to accept the hypothesis that Bardesanes strongly modified Brahmanic theology under the influence of his Syrian Christianity, linked to Gnosis and Platonism.[75] The description of the god cannot be defined as Bardesanes's fantasy,[76] for we have discovered a lot of corresponding particulars in Indian sculptures. The series of symbols of everything that covered the body of the god has no precise model in Ardhanarisvara's iconography, and therefore Cristiano Castelletti sought it in several statues of the "cosmological Buddha,"[77] whose garments are decorated by symbols of the cosmic order. Instead, the gem points, rather, toward Shiva's iconography and the head, which is encircled by sunbeams, depends not only on the solar theology of the western provinces, but also on the doctrines of the *Upanishads*.[78]

Leaving these topics aside, it is worth noting that the Brahmans in Syria or Mesopotamia were aware of Platonic theology and other streams of Western thought. They inspired the gem cutter or inspired one wise man, or a Magus, who gave the gem cutter a drawing of the androgynous god in front of the creator. We do not know whether Brahmans or their pupils modified the Indian iconographical models so as to merge them with Platonic or Gnostic ideas.

Aristoxenos the Peripatetic imagined a meeting between Socrates and a Brahman, who taught Socrates the identity of man and divine nature.[79] The Brahmans' ability to teach in Greek cannot be ruled out, because in India many Greek kings ruled after Alexander the Great and after the foundation of an independent Greek kingdom in Bactria under Diodotos I (3rd century BC). The tradition of Milinda-Menandros (second half of the 2nd century BC)[80] discussing philosophy with Buddhist wise men proves

---

[75] R. Reitzenstein, H.H. Schaeder, *Studien zum antiken Synkretismus aus Iran und Griechenland*, Studien der Bibliothek Warburg, 7 (Leipzig: Teubner, 1926), 64–72; F. Winter, *Bardesanes von Edessa über Indien*, Frühes Christentum 5 (Thaur bei Innsbruck: Druck und Verlagshaus Thaur, 1999), 64, 73–82.

[76] As has been supposed by Reitzenstein and Schaeder, 91–92; *contra*: Castelletti, 257.

[77] On which, see A. Falco Howard, *The Imagery of the Cosmological Buddha* (Leiden: Brill, 1986); Castelletti, 257–61.

[78] Another gem in Paris [A. Delatte, Ph. Derchain, *Les intailles magiques gréco-égyptiennes* (Paris: Bibliothèque Nationale, 1964), no. 143] depicts Harpokrates with two signs on the left breast.

[79] Pseudo-Aristoteles, *Magikòs*, fr. 32 Rose (= Diogenes Laertius II.45); J. Festugière, "Trois rencontres entre l'Inde et l'Occident" and "Grecs et Sages orientaux", in *Etudes de philosophie grecque* (Paris: J. Vrin, 1971), 157–95.

[80] *Milindapanha: Les questions de Milinda*, trans. from Pâli by L. Finot (Paris: Editions Dharma, 1923).

the possibility of profound exchanges between these two cultures. A century before Menandros, Ashoka (first half of the 3rd century BC) wrote letters to Macedonian kings in Greece, Syria, Libya, and Egypt to explain Buddhist ethics.[81] The possibility of learning Indian philosophy and religion was open to the Greeks.

Furthermore, we are not at all sure that the gem was produced in Syria, because Damascius says that a group of Brahmans once went to Alexandria[82] and it is possible that some influences of Brahmanic thought were also accepted in Egypt. The gem in the British Museum described in this chapter (see Figure 3.5, p. 73), depicting Harpokrates with a snake, is similar to the gem in Naples. A Gandharan relief from Swât shows a human being on a lotus flower and indicates an influence of Harpokrates's iconography on Buddhist imagery.[83] These facts suggest that Egypt could have played a role in the gem's iconography. Therefore it is possible that a Platonizing theologist influenced by Indian ideas ordered the gem from an engraver, who was used to producing gems engraved with the image of Harpokrates.

Knowledge of Indian theologies was gotten through the teachings of the Brahmans and readings of some books. Another way was knowing the iconographies of Indian gods. The best known example of this is found in the ivory statue that represents the goddess Lakshmi, which was discovered at Pompei.[84] Contact between India and the Roman Empire was exceedingly frequent during the Severan period, when the Parthian

---

[81] J. Bloch, *Les inscriptions d'Asoka* (Paris: Les Belles Lettres, 1950), 130; G. Pugliese Carratelli, *Gli editti di Ashoka* (Milano: Adelphi, 2003).

[82] *Vita Isidori*, p. 96 Zintzen. An Indian origin of the gem is out of the question because of the quite correct engraving of the Greek inscription on the reverse. A few magical gems are supposed to come from India [C.W. King, *The Gnostics and their Remains* (London: Bell and Daldy, 1887), 297–302; C. Bonner, "Amulets chiefly in the British Museum," *Hesperia* 20 (1951): 308] but their antiquity is under suspicion. Traces of the activity of gem-engraving workshops have been discovered at Vîrapatnam, near Pondichéry, where a cornaline that depicts Augustus has been found: see J. Filliozat, "Les échanges de l'Inde et de l'Empire romain aux premiers siècles de l'ère chrétienne", *Revue Historique* 201 (1949): 18. Additionally, the Indian workshops also produced imitations of Roman artifacts: Filliozat, 22–23. The Indian iconography of the Decans was influenced by hellenistic iconography: D. Pingree, "The Indian Iconography of the Decans and Horâs," *JWCI* 26 (1963): 233–54.

[83] M. Taddei, "Harpocrates, Brahmâ, Maitreya. A tentative interpretation of a Gandharan relief from Swât," *Dialoghi di Archeologia* 3 (1969), 364–90.

[84] A. Maiuri, "Statuetta eburnea d'arte indiana a Pompei", *Le Arti* (dicembre-gennaio 1938), 111, plate XLII–XLV; see Filliozat, "Les échanges de l'Inde et de l'Empire romain", 13–25. Referring to the possible influence of the Graeco-Buddhist art of northern India on Severan art: M. Grant, *The Severans. The Changed Roman Empire* (London: Routledge, 1996), 61; and on possible relations between Greek and Roman and Burmese glyptics: S.E. Hoey Middleton, *Intaglios, Cameos, Rings and Related Objects from Burma and Java. The White Collection and a Further Small Collection by Robert Wilkins* (Oxford: BAR international series, 2005). On the similarities between Cynic philosophers and Indian Brahmans, see G. Bodei Giglioni, "Una leggenda sulle origini dell'ellenismo. Alessandro e i cinici", in *Studi ellenistici*, I, ed. B. Virgilio (Pisa: Giardini, 1984), 51–73.

reign was weakened by military débâcles. This is proved by the discovery of a number of Severan aurei, and even their local imitations, which have been found in India.[85]

Through the examination of these gems we know of another exceptional case of an interaction between theologies. As claimed by Flavius Philostratus,[86] the Indian Brahmans taught that the cosmos was a living being that was made up of both sexes, which loved each other and thus created the cosmos itself.

The attitude of the creator on the gem recalls that of theurgists during their performances. In fact, Michael Psellus, commenting on a fragment of the Chaldaean Oracles, writes:

> As they [the theurgists] whirled them [magical golden balls called *iynges*], they uttered random sounds, or sounds like an animal, laughing and lashing the air. [The Oracle] teaches that the movement of the top, having an ineffable power, accomplishes the rite.[87]

"Theurgist" meant "he who is acting like a god."[88] Theurgists did use whips, roared like animals, and also used axes, so as to imitate the creator god, whose image is depicted on the Naples gem. One could therefore suppose that the gem corresponds to Indian theological ideas merged with some features of theurgical religion. Moreover, one has to admit that the Gnostic ideas shared similar features of the animal-like creator, who was inspired by the vision of supreme realities. According to Gnostic ideas—as we have seen— the supreme divinities were androgynous.[89]

Having ascertained the Indian influence on the iconography of that gem, it is possible to put forward a hypothetical interpretation of the inscription *charkandabraê* as a (partially) Sanskrit word, which surrounds the god's head. In Sanskrit *cakra* signifies "disk, wheel, circle,"[90] but the rest, *dabraê*, has no meaning. It is possible to add that the word

---

[85] P. Berghaus Peter, "Felicitas saeculi in Indien", in *MOYΣIKOΣ ANHP. Festschrift für Max Wegner zum 90. Geburtstag*, eds., Oliver Brehm and Sascha Klie (Bonn: Habelt, 1992), 11–16.

[86] *Vita Apollonii* III.34.

[87] Psellus, *Opuscula* 38 (*Philosophica minora*, II, ed. D.I. O'Meara 133); cf. A. Mastrocinque, "The Divinatory Kit from Pergamon and Greek Magic in Late Antiquity," *Journal of Roman Archaeology* 15 (2002): 174–87.

[88] See B. Pearson, "Theurgic Tendencies in Gnosticism and Iamblichus' Conception of Theurgy," in *Neoplatonism and Gnosticism*, eds. R.T. Wallis and J. Bregman (Albany: State University of New York Press, 1992), 255; cf. F. Cremer, *Die chaldäischen Orakel und Jamblichus de mysteriis* (Meisenheim am Glan: Anton Hain, 1969), 21–22; Mastrocinque, "The Divinatory Kit from Pergamon," 186–87.

[89] Brisson, *Le sexe incertain*, 92–95. On the Theurgists who imitated the creator god, see G. Shaw, *Theurgy and the Soul: The Neoplatonism of Iamblichus* (University Park, PA: Pennsylvania State University Press, 1995), part 5; J.P. Anton, "Theurgia-demiourgia: A Controversial Issue in Hellenistic Thought and Religion," in *Neoplatonism and Gnosticism*, eds. Wallis and Bregman, 9–31.

[90] I am grateful to Thomas Malten of the University of Cologne for his advice.

XAPXEN∆ABPAH seems to be similar to AKPAKANAPBA, a *vox* that is used in an apollinean magical recipe.[91]

We are used to giving gems such as the one in Naples the title of "magic" and to assuming "magic" to be the source of inspiration for both the iconography and the inscriptions. Actually, the thinker who conceived this amulet had a rich and profound knowledge of theology and philosophy. He was active during the same period as Origenes, Julius Africanus, and Bardesanes, who were tracing new paths in the field of religion. He was looking for a synthesis among the highest theological speculations, such as Platonic, Jewish, Indian, and maybe theurgical ones. The classification of such gems as "magic" is the result of a judgment, a judgment that derives from a biased opposition between magic and religion that occurred during the Roman Empire. The strongest supporters of such an opposition were the Christian apologists, whose points of view had been accepted by Roman Christian emperors and jurists.[92]

## ANOTHER POSSIBLE CONTEMPLATING CREATOR

The passage by Porphyry continues by saying:

> He (Bardesanes) says that he has made an inquiry about the statue's material. Sandales asserted and others claimed that nobody knew the nature of this material. In fact it was not of gold nor of silver, bronze or stone, it is rather similar to hard wood and absolutely free from putridity. But it is not wood. They added that one king wanted to pull out one of the hairs from around the neck, but blood flowed and the king got so scared that with difficulty he got over the shock thanks to the prayers of Brahmans.
>
> They say that on the statue's head there is apparently a statue of a god sitting on a throne.

From this passage we learn that the statue was hairy, so we can presume that this "hairiness" describes the male half. One hairy god is represented on a gem together with another creator god, Chnoumis.

1. In fact, in the British Museum there is a yellow jasper gem (Figure 3.8)[93] on which a divinity is represented in a static position. It is an anthropomorphic hairy animal, with short legs, open arms, and raised

---

[91] *PGM* II, 65, where the word had to be repeated eleven times, eliminating a letter each time.

[92] On this opposition see Mastrocinque, *From Jewish Magic*, §§ 64–67.

[93] Michel, *British Museum*, no. 156. J.F. Quack, review of Michel, *British Museum*, *Gnomon* 76 (2004): 262, suspects this gem and all those depicting this god are fakes. Actually there are no grounds for seriously raising such a doubt.

Figure 3.8   Yellow jasper in the British Museum, London, representing a hairy god and the snake Chnoubis.

Reproduced by courtesy of the Trustees of the British Museum.

forearms. Its body is frontal; its ears are pointed; its open hands are human and are placed under two stars. Over its head a snake is raised, the snake's head is decorated with a palm branch. On the left side the name XNOYMIE and the Chnoubis's sign (SSS barred by one central line) are cut. Chnoumis, or Chnoubis, is a peculiar form of the Egyptian creator god Chnum, whose snake's body has a lion's head. This god is represented on the right side of the gem, coiled and looking up to the tall god. On the reverse side the inscription is: ΗΛΙΑΜΒΡΩ ΑΒΡΑΜΑΩΘ ΑΝΟΧ (Eliambrô Abramaôth Anoch).

2. The same god is depicted on another gem (Figure 3.9) made of the same material, which is kept in the Skolouda collection.[94] In this case its arms are almost completely open, its head is that of a dog, it is ithyphallic and standing on bended legs. It is alone and the inscription on the reverse is: ΗΛΙΑΒΡΩ ΝΗΜΕΜΟΡΩ ΠΟΙΗΣΑΤΕ ΑΠΟΝΟΝ ΤΟΝ ΣΤΟΜΑΧΟΝ ΜΑΡΙΑΝ (Eliambrô Nênemorô free Maria from stomach pains).

3. The same god is depicted on another yellow jasper in the Staatliche Münzsammlung in Munich.[95] Here the inscription ends with . . . ΧΑΡΧ-ΑΡΝΑΙΒΑΩΣ, which could recall the word ΧΑΡΧΕΝΔΑΒΡΑΗ on the rays of the god of the gem from Naples.

---

[94] S. Michel, *Bunte Steine—Dunkle Bilder: Magische Gemmen* (Munich: Biering & Brinkmann, 2001), no. 142.

[95] E. Brandt, A. Krug, W. Gercke, and E. Schmidt, *AGDS I, München* (München: Prestel, 1972), no. 2899.

**Figure 3.9** Yellow jasper in the Skoluda collection, Hamburg, representing a hairy god (photograph by S. Michel).

Reprinted with the permission of S. Michel.

4. Another specimen is found in the Cabinet des Médailles in Paris[96]; its inscription is ΗΛΙΑΜΒΡΩ (Figure 3.10).

5. A red jasper in the British Museum[97] depicts the same god and has the inscription: ΗΛΙΑΜΒΡΩ (Figure 3.11).

There are two possible interpretations of this gem: two gods (Chnoumis and the hairy god) are simply coupled so as to join their forces in the same amulet, or they are represented in a specific attitude toward each other. We have no sure means of choosing either interpretation. In the second case, the creator, Chnum, is contemplating the image of a static god.

The heresiologist Hippolytos[98] reports the doctrine of a Christian "heretical" sect, the Naassenes (the "worshippers of the snake"), focusing especially on their belief in the Anthropos, the "perfect divine Man," the first

---

[96] Delatte, Derchain, no. 435. Perhaps also the obsidian published by S. Hoey Middleton, *Seals, Finger Rings, Engraved Gems and Amulets in the Royal Albert Memorial Museum, Exeter* (Exeter: Exeter City Museums, 1998), 67–68, no. 54 (on the other side there is a snake with a janiform head).

[97] Michel, *British Museum*, no. 157.

[98] *Refutatio haeresium* V.8.9-10, trans. J.H. MacMahon. On the Hippolytos passage describing the Naassene doctrine, see M.G. Lancellotti, *The Naassenes. A Gnostic Identity among Judaism, Christianity, Classical and Ancient Near Eastern Traditions* (Münster: Ugarit-Verlag, 2000).

**Figure 3.10A**  Yellow jasper in the Cabinet des Médailles, Paris, representing a hairy god (photograph by the author).

Reproduced with the permission of the Cabinet des Médailles.

manifestation of the unknowable god. The speculation of the Naassenes looked for traces of such a god in the pagan tradition and through the mysteries of Samothracia they found a record of such a divine manifestation. The Father of the Church writes that the Naassene is dealing with

> the great and ineffable mystery of the Samothracians, which it is allowable— he says—for us only who are initiated to know. For the Samothra-

90

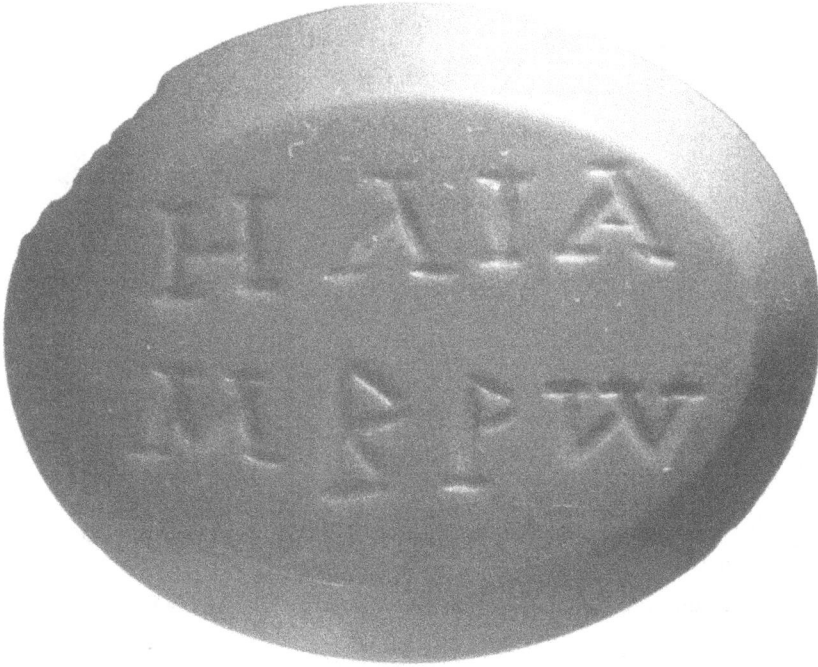

**Figure 3.10B**   Reverse side.

cians expressly hand down, in the mysteries that are celebrated among
them, Adam[99] as the primal man. Habitually there stand in the temple of
the Samothracians two images of naked men, having both hands stretched
aloft towards heaven, and their pudenda erecta, as with the statue of
Mercury on Mount Cyllene.

It is possible (but far from certain) that the ithyphallic and cynocephalic
god[100] on the gems is Mercury/Hermes in his Egyptian form. The Egyptian
Hermes was Thoth, who had two main iconographies, either as a baboon
or as an ibis. The cynocephalic ape is often represented on magical gems
with raised arms and a phallus, in adoration of the sun god Harpokrates.
The interpretation of the gem as the creator in contemplation of the
Anthropos is probable.

If we want to take a step further in the same direction, we notice the
little snake on the Anthropos's head. Its position is the same as the small

---

[99] Or Adamna; see D.M. Cosi, "Adamma. Un problema e qualche proposta", *Atti e Memorie
dell'Accademia Patavina* 88/3 (1975–76): 149–56.

[100] According to S. Michel it is, in fact, the baboon in anthropomorphic form.

**Figure 3.11** Red jasper in the British Museum, London, representing a hairy god and the snake Chnoubis.

Reproduced by courtesy of the Trustees of the British Museum.

god on the head of the Indian god. In this case, it is often assumed that it represented the river Ganges over the head of Ardhanarisvara. Sometimes the images of Shiva show a furious old woman twisted in the hair of the god; she is Gangâ, the personification of the Indian river.[101] In Western thought such a goddess could not have a meaning. According to Bardesanes and Porphyry, instead of this woman, a god on a throne was represented. One image of Ardhanarisvara shows him with a snake in his hair.[102] The little snake on the gems could represent the snake-god of the Northern pole of the heaven, the divine supreme god, according to some Gnostic religious streams.[103] In this case, the cynocephalic Anthropos was raising his hands and his phallus toward this god. Obviously, other interpretations are possible.

The simple use of these amulets, which were cut for the health of the stomach and other organs, should not lead us to underestimate the theological speculation that supports the daily use of amulets.

---

[101] Yadav, 26–27; Castelletti, 264. Epiphanius, *De Gemmis: The Old Georgian Version and the Fragments of the Armenian Version*, by R. P. Blakez and *the Coptic-Sahidic Fragments*, by H. De Vis (London: Christophers, 1934), 107, 111, and 131, mentions precious stones that were found in the Ganges.

[102] Yadav, Fig. C.11; cf. Fig. A.

[103] Mastrocinque, *From Jewish Magic*, § 45–48, 59.

# CONCLUSION

It it wise to limit the conclusion of this research to the discovery of Brahmanic theological influences on Western religious speculation on the supreme god and the creator. Communication between Brahmans and people of the Roman Empire would not have been exceptional, even though it was very rare to have the opportunity of bringing together a thinker like Bardesanes and Indian wise men. According to the fabulous story of Apollonius of Tyana by Flavius Philostratus,[104] this Pythagorean prophet once went to India and met the Brahmans. They gave him seven rings, on which the names of seven planets were cut, and he wore these rings alternately during the week.

It is very probable that this story is only a fable, but readers of Philostratus accepted it as a possibility. The gem in the Museum of Naples shows that such magical stones were produced under the influence of Indian Brahmanic doctrines. In this way the divine Anthropos, the supreme Idea produced by the unknowable and higher god to give a model to creation, was proposed in the Indian style.

---

[104] *Vita Apollonii* III.41.

.

# Chapter 4

# ASKLEPIOS LEONTOUCHOS AND DIVINE TRIADS ON SYRIAN GEMS

# ONE ARABIAN DIVINE TRIAD AND
# ONE FROM HIERAPOLIS

Magical gems are not exclusively a product of Roman Egypt. Syria and neighboring areas played an important role in their production. Several years ago Glen Bowersock[1] produced a short study about an inscribed jasper gem that was seen by Wilhelm Froehner in Nazareth.[2] The inscription on the gem is:

ΑΡΗΣ
ΘΕΑΝΔΡΟΣΟ
ΔΟΥΣΑΡΗ
ΝΟΥΑΕΜΙΘ
ΗΡΑΣΘΗ
ΡΑΒΟΝ

In the fourth line a feminine Semitic name can be recognized: Νουλεμιθ, or better Σουλεμιθ: šlmt. Ραβος is a male Semitic name, and line 5 contains a verb, ἡράσθη, "is loved." Therefore Bowersock suggests a magical use for the gem in an erotic context. This fact isolates the three names on lines 1–3 as those of a divine triad: Ares, Theandr(i)os, and Dusare(s). The coinage of the city of Bostra under the Roman Emperors Elagabalus, Decius, and Etruscilla depicts two baetyls (sacred stones supposed to be endowed with life and to be seats of gods) and bears the name of Dusares. The name of the second baetyl could be one of those on the gem.

This is not a singular case among magical gems; we know of a few specimens that depict triads from cities of the Near East, and the joint study of gems and coins allows a good understanding of the local civic cults. Indeed, the coinage of a number of Near Eastern cities depicts local gods, which are sometimes organized in triads.

Another example is that of a hematite from Seyrig's collection[3] (Figure 4.1), now in the Cabinet des Médailles, and bought at Aleppo. The form of this intaglio is very similar to a small kidney. Pliny the Elder[4] knew of a stone called "Adad's kidney"; it is highly probable that this stone was

---

[1] G. Bowersock. "An Arabian Trinity," *HTR* 79 (1986): 17–21.

[2] W. Froener, *Mélanges d'épigraphie et d'archéologie* (Paris: Detaille, 1875); cf. L. Robert, *Collection Froehner* (Paris: Éditions des Bibliothèques Nationales, 1936), 115, n. 3; D. Sourdel, *Les cultes du Hauran à l'époque romaine* (Paris: Imprimerie Nationale, 1952), 77, n. 2; G.W. Bowersock, "The Arabian Ares," in *Tria corda: Scritti in onore di Arnaldo Momigliano* (Como: New Press, 1983), 44, n. 3.

[3] H. Seyrig, "Antiquités syriennes. 40. Sur une idole hiérapolitaine", *Syria* 26 (1949): 17–28; H.J.W. Drijvers, *Cults and Beliefs at Edessa*, EPRO 82 (Leiden: Brill, 1980), 32 and plate XXXIV.3.

[4] *Naturalis historia* XXXVII.186: *Adadu nep<h>ros <sive> renes, eiusdem oculus, digitus; deus et hic colitur a Syris.* See A.A. Barb, "Lapis Adamas", in *Hommages à Marcel Renard*, I (Bruxelles: Latomus, 1969), 72.

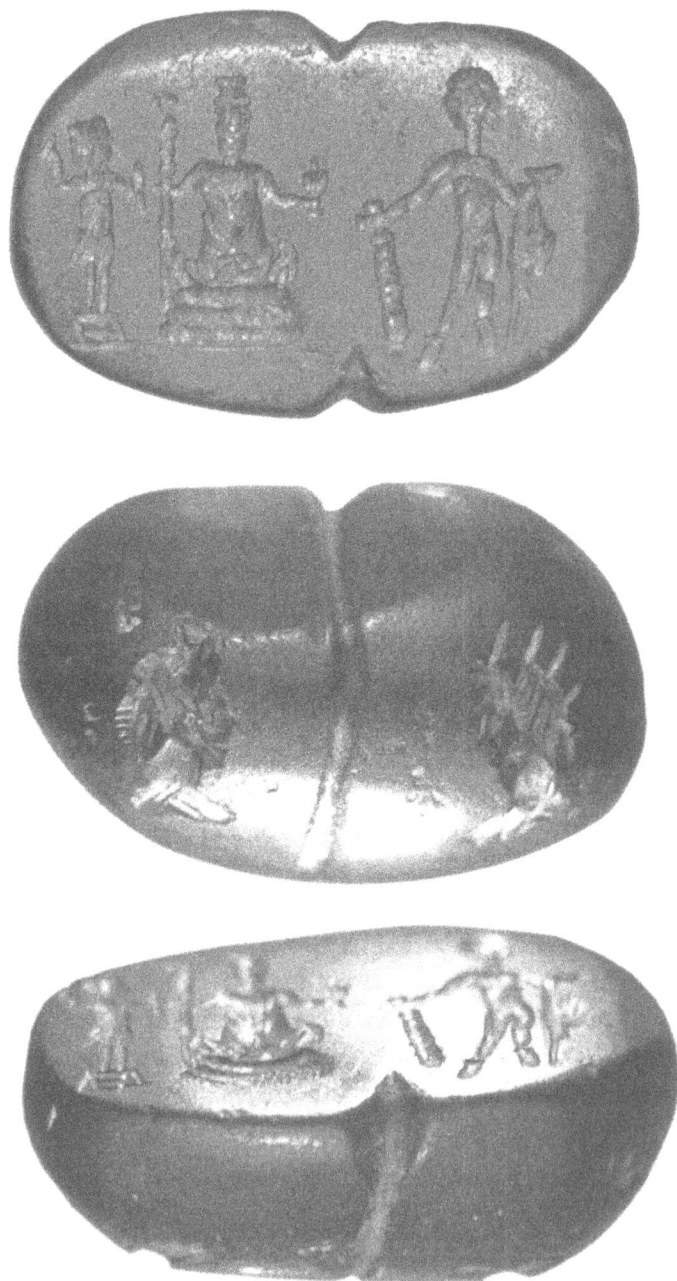

**Figure 4.1** Hematite intaglio in the Cabinet des Médailles, Paris, representing a Syrian divine triad (photograph by the author).

Reproduced with the permission of the Cabinet des Médailles.

hematite or limonite. On the flat side three gods are engraved, namely, a smiting god, maybe Adad; the idol of Apollo[5] of Hierapolis–Bambyke (Syria); and Heracles. The reverse side shows Selene and Helios. Between them an engraved line divides the stone into two areas, in the same way as on divinatory terracotta or bronze Etruscan livers, where the line represents a boundary between favorable and hostile zones. The *Orphei lithika kerygmata*[6] mention the mantic properties of siderite, a sort of hematite, and therefore one cannot exclude a mantic purpose for this intaglio.

Henry Seyrig[7] has recognized the peculiar statue of Apollo on this coin thanks to a tetradrachm struck in Hierapolis under Caracalla—his shield is decorated with the image of the local Apollinean idol.[8] Cultic statues of this kind recur only in Syria and Palestine.[9]

## A TRIAD OF ASCALON ON A GEM KEPT IN VERONA

The most important case we present here concerns the touchstone gem (Figure 4.2) in the Civic Museum of Verona at Castel Vecchio.[10] Its origins are unknown and the gem was previously kept in the collection of Count Verità. This rich collection was acquired by the municipality in 1842. The style of the engraving would suggest a date in the 2nd or 3rd century CE On its surface, from left to right, one can see: an Egyptian god standing and holding a *nekhekh* whip and a *was* sceptre. He wears a wig that is decorated with a disc and a large *atef* crown. He is accompanied by three lions walking to the right. Tyche is standing at the center, holding the cornucopia with her left hand and a bird with the right. A small crown, formed by two lines, is on her head. It is the same type of crown that usually adorns Isis's head on the gems of Imperial times. Perseus is standing on the right, holding the *harpe* in his raised right hand; he holds a round shield (rather than the bag to hide Medusa's head) with his left. Behind the shield there is a palm branch. His head bears a Phrygian or Persian hat; on his legs he wears *anaxyrides* (trousers worn by Eastern nations).

---

[5] On which: Macrobius I.17.66–67.

[6] 18, 156–7 Halleux-Schamp.

[7] Seyrig, "Antiquités syriennes. 40."

[8] H. Seyrig, "Antiquités syriennes. 11. Sur certains tétradrachmes provinciaux de Syrie", *Syria* 13, (1932): 360–62.

[9] See the coins of Dium, in the Decapolis: W. Wroth, *Catalogue of the Greek Coins of Galatia, Cappadocia, and Syria* (London: Longmans, 1899), 303, nos. 1–2, plate XXXVIII.4.

[10] E. Gagetti, in *387 a.C. Ambrogio e Agostino. Le sorgenti dell'Europa*, Catalogo della mostra (Milano: Olivares, 2003), 440, n. 335 and cat. 334 (where the divine triad is identified as Magna Mater, Tyche, and Attis); *SGG* II, VR 28. The dimensions are cm 1.6 x 1.3 x 0.2; the inventory no. is 25394.

**Figure 4.2**    Touchstone gem in the Civic Museum at Castel Vecchio, Verona, representing a triad of gods of Ascalon (photograph by the author).

Reproduced with the permission of the Civic Museum at Castel Vecchio.

The first and third gods provide us with the details we need to recognize the triads as typical of Ascalon.

## PERSEUS

In considering the gem shown in Figure 4.2 first we will deal with Perseus. This gem allows us to recognize the hero, or god, who is present on several bronze coins issued by the city of Ascalon (Figure 4.3), which is accompanied by the inscription: Phanebalos.[11] In the past the interpretation

---

[11] G.F. Hill, *Catalogue of the Greek Coins of Palestine (Galilee, Samaria, and Judaea)* (London: Longmans, 1914 = *BMCPalestine*), 115, nos. 74–80, plate XIII.7 (Augustus); 118–19, nos. 95–103, plates XIII.11–12 (Nero); 120, nos. 109–16 (Vespasian); 122–23, nos. 128–35 (Domitian); 125–26, nos. 158–68 (Trajan); 128–29, nos. 181–90, plates XIII.18–19 (Hadrian); 133–34, nos. 216–25, plates XIV.4-5 (Antoninus Pius); 138, no. 242, plate XIV.13; (Elagabalus) 139, nos. 246–47, plate XIV.14 (Severus Alexander) the nos. 188 and 216-218 bear the inscription: ΑΣ(ΚΑΛΩΝ) ΦΑΝΗΒΑΛ; no. 216: ΑΣ(ΚΑΛΩΝ) ΦΑΝΗΒΑΛΟΣ. For the reign of Caligula, Claudius, and Nero: A. Burnett, M. Amandry, P.P. Ripollès, *Roman Provincial Coinage*, I.1 (London-Paris: British Museum Press, 1992), 674 and 676, nos. 4884, 4886, 4889, and 4892. This god is also represented on a lead seal from Ascalon: R.P. Declœdt, "Plombs du Musée Biblique de Sainte-Anne de Jérusalem", *Revue Numismatique* (1914): 422–23. F. Imhoof-Blumer, "Zur griechischen und römischen Münzkunde", *Rev. Suisse de Num.* 14 (1908): 129–30, first recognized the *harpe*, which is the well-known weapon of Perseus. See also E. Lipinski, *Dieux et déesses de l'univers phénicien* (Leuven: Peeters, 1995), 200–1.

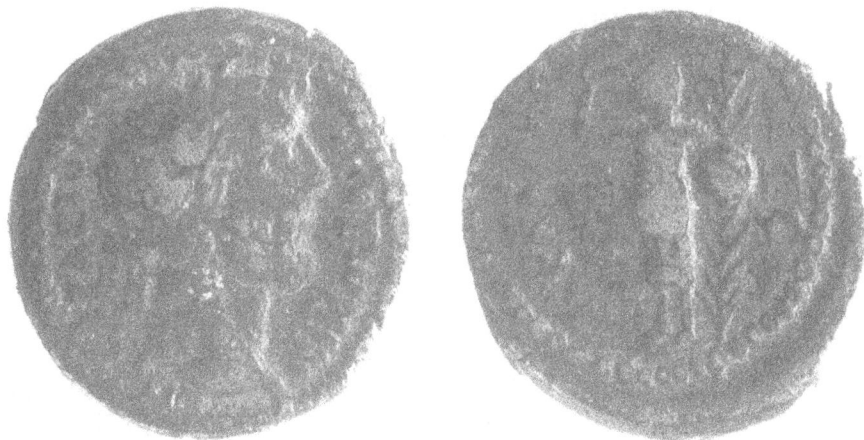

**Figure 4.3** Bronze coin of Ascalon, from the era of Antoninus Pius, representing Phanebalos.

Reproduced from Internet auction catalogues.

of this hero's image has been controversial but the gem is very clear in depicting the characteristic sword of Perseus and garments rendered in Persian style. Many cities of Southern Phoenicia and Palestine, especially Ioppe,[12] venerated the Greek hero, who was believed to be an ancestor of the Persians.[13] In Egypt too Perseus was greatly respected, especially in the Theban district.[14] Fishermen of the Erythrean sea called a big fish "Perseus,"[15] clearly remembering the myth of Perseus and Danae recovered by the fishermen of Seryphos, as told in Aeschylos's *Diktylkoi*.[16] Scenes and characters of the myth of Perseus were popular in Anatolia, especially during the Persian domination, as has been proved by the pictures of Elmalı in Lycia or by the cult of Chrysaor in eastern Caria. In the late 4th century BC on Samarian silver issues, the Gorgoneion and Pegasus were represented.[17] The Gorgon was the monster that Perseus beheaded and Pegasus was the horse that was engendered by the Gorgon and the brother of Chrysaor. Robin Lane Fox correctly stated that "Perseus became the hero of integration between East and West."[18] The antiquity of the

---

[12] Iosephus, *Bellum Iudaicum* III.420; Plinius, *Naturalis historia* V.128; Pausanias IV.35.9.

[13] Herodotus I.125; VI.54

[14] Herodotus II.91; see S.Sauneron, "Persée, dieu de Khemmis", *Rev. d'Ég.* 14, 1962, 53- 57.

[15] Aelianus, *De natura animalium* III.28; Hesychius, s.v. *Persos*.

[16] TGF, III, F 46–47.

[17] G. Chaya, "The Samarian Greek Gorgoneion Coin Series," *Israel Numismatic Journal* 14 (2000–2002): 19–25.

[18] R. Lane Fox, *Alexander the Great* (London: Allen Lane, 1973), 201.

cult of Perseus in the Near East and Egypt proves that many local gods were identified with Perseus and received his iconography. The Persian Empire was probably the catalyst for such a widespread phenomenon.

The local name of the Greek hero, Phanebalos, and the bad quality of coin engraving engendered some misunderstanding about this protagonist of Ascalonite mythology. The name derives from the Greek rendering of the semitic *pn b'l*, "Face of Baal."[19] This name is typical of Tanit as is stated in many inscriptions of Carthaginian territory.[20] Consequently, a hypothesis has been proposed according to which the god on the Ascalonite coins is Tanit herself.[21] A sign in the form of the Greek Δ with a bar above, on a bronze coin issued under Hadrian[22] has been taken as a proof of this identification.[23] However, one has to admit that it is impossible to identify a god with *harpe* and Persian dress as Tanit. Reinhold Merkelbach and Maria Totti recognized a similar expression in the words φον Θώθ of the 7th magical papyrus,[24] whose meaning could be "face of Thoth." Another occurrence of the same expression is found on a magical axe.[25]

Javier Teixidor[26] underlined that Phanebal signifies "face, or presence of Baal," and that Astarte was named ΣΑΜΑΒΩΛΩ, *sm b'l*, "name of Baal" at Ugarit and Tyros.[27] He supposed also that Phanebalos was identified with Apollo.[28] In Egypt it was very common to call a deity "the soul, the heart . . . of another god." For instance, Apis was the soul of Osiris. In the magical name of Thoth, σαλβαναχαμβρη, D. Wortmann[29] recog-

[19] As first recognized by G.F. Hill, "Some Palestinian Cults in the Graeco-Roman Age," *Proc. of the British Academy* 5 (1912): 422, who also rightly stated that the image was that of a male god. He preferred to identify him with Baal-Zeus.

[20] See C.L. Seow, "Face," in *Dictionary of Deities and Demons in the Bible* (Leiden: Brill, 1995), columns 607–9.

[21] G. Finkielsztejn, "Phanebal, déesse d'Ascalon" in *Numismatique et histoire économique phéniciennes et puniques*, eds. T. Hackens and G. Moucharte, Actes du Colloque tenu a Louvain-la-Neuve, 13-16 mai 1987 (Studia Phoenicia 9) (Louvain: Université Catholique de Louvain, 1992), 51–58. This author believes that Phanebalos was the Phoenician Tanit, similar to Astarte. The gem actually proves that Astarte of Ascalon was different from Phanebalos. Finkielsztejn's hypothesis has been rejected by G. Fuks, "Cults and Deities in Hellenistic and Roman Ashkelon," *Mediterranean Historical Review* 15.2 (2000): 27–48, part. 32–35. R. Dussaud, *Notes de mythologie syrienne* (Paris: Leroux, 1905), 76–79, thought that this god was Heracles-Bel and was identified with Dagan, the corn god; *contra*: G.F. Hill, "Some Palestinian Cults," 422. H. Seyrig, "Les dieux armés et les Arabes de Syrie," *Syria* 47, (1970): 77–100, part. 96–97, supposed that Phanebalos was of Arabian origin, in consideration of the Arabian origin of many warrior gods in Syria.

[22] Hill, *BMC Palaestine*, p. 129 (a very badly preserved specimen).

[23] M. Dothan, "A Sign of Tanit from Tell 'Akko'," *IEJ* 24 (1974): 44–9, part. 46.

[24] *PGM* VII.500; see R. Merkelbach and M. Totti, *Abrasax. Ausgewählte Papyri religiösen und magischen Inhalts*, I, Papyrologica Coloniensia 17.1 (Opladen: Westdeutsche Verlag, 1990), 101.

[25] A. Mastrocinque, *Studi sul Mitraismo. Il Mitraismo e la magia* (Roma: Giorgio Bretschneider, 1998), chapter VII.

[26] "Bulletin d'épigraphie sémitique", in *Syria* 49 (1972): 423, n. 62.

[27] J. Teixidor, *The Pantheon of Palmyra*, EPRO 79 (Leiden: Brill, 1979), 59.

[28] J. Teixidor, *Pagan Gods* (Princeton, NJ: Princeton University Press, 1977), 96–97.

[29] D. Wortmann, "Kosmogonie und Nilflut", *Bonner Jahrbücher* 166 (1966): 98, n. 256.

**Figure 4.4** Green jasper gem in the National Archaeological Museum, Florence, representing a lion-headed god who beheaded Gorgo (photograph by the author).

Reproduced with the permission of the National Archaeological Museum.

nized an Egyptian expression signifying "living heart of Re." The Jewish tradition knew the hand, the arm, the feet, the wisdom, the word of God—in the Imperial Age many of these divine manifestations were worshipped as independent gods. Also Perseus of Ascalon was a major god of Ascalon. His relation to Baal was probably similar to that of the Greek hero to Zeus: His son. The cult of Perseus was a peculiar Near-Eastern and

Egyptian feature, whereas the Greeks gave him minor importance. In consideration of the antiquity of the spreading of the cult of Perseus in Anatolia, Palestine, Samaria, and Egypt, one cannot exclude that any feature of his myth had been borrowed by the Greeks from an Eastern culture. Furthermore, Perseus earned an important place in the religious doctrines that could be defined as non-Christian gnosis.[30] The leontocephalic warrior god, who was called Ialdabaoth or Sabaoth, was sometimes depicted as Medusa's conqueror. On several gems he is holding the monster's head and a sword[31] (Figure 4.4). Another gem bears an inscription that mentions Perseus as he who pursues the demon of pellagra.[32]

## ASKLEPIOS WITH THE LIONS

A lead tessera from Ascalon depicts Phanebalos, Asklepios, and Hygieia.[33] Therefore, it is evident that the physician god was worshipped with the Greek hero. In Ascalon, Asclepios had very peculiar features: he was a god accompanied by three lions.

The god with three lions and Egyptian dress is typical of the Ascalonite pantheon, which has been recently studied by Nicole Belayche.[34] His image recurs on the coins of that city[35] (Figures 4.5 and 4.6) and on six gems.[36]

---

[30] A. Mastrocinque, *From Jewish Magic to Gnosticism*, Studien und Texte zu Antike und Christentum 24, (Tübingen: Mohr-Siebeck, 2005), 70–85.

[31] *SGG* II, Fi 44 (here, Fig. 4.4); A. Mastrocinque, "Studies in Gnostic Gems: The Gem of Judah," *Journal for the Study of Judaism* 33.2 (2002): 164–70; see also the yellow jasper, Michel, *British Museum*, no. 276.

[32] O. Neverov, *Antique Intaglios in the Hermitage Collection* (Leningrad: Aurora, 1976), no. 143a.

[33] S. Ronzevalle, "Notes et études d'archéologie orientale—Hélioséros", *MUB* 16 (1932): 14–15 (who supposes that Phanebalos is construed with Phanes, the Orphic god, and Baal, and identifies Asklepios with the Osiriform god depicted on the coins). E. Friedheim, *Rabbinisme et Paganisme en Palestine romaine*, RGRW 157 (Leiden: Brill, 2006), 239, identifies Phanebalos with Asklepios, but there is no doubt that they were two different gods.

[34] N. Belayche, *Iudaea-Palaestina. The Pagan Cults in Roman Palestine (Second to Fourth Century)* (Tübingen: Mohr-Siebeck, 2001), 220–32.

[35] *BMC Palestine*, 131, nos. 202–205 (Antoninus Pius); 137, no. 234 (Geta); 138, no. 134 (Elagabalus). His bust over three lions on other coins: p. 140, nos. 251–252, plate XIV.15–16 (Maximinus Trax). Since Hill's publication, other coins have been discovered: Y. Meshorer, *City-Coins of Eretz Israel and the Decapolis in the Roman Period* (Jerusalem: The Israel Museum, 1985), 111, no. 52 (Marcus Aurelius); *SNG AMNS*, VI, no. 734, plate 22; M. Rosenberger, *The Rosenberger Israel Collection*, I: *Aelia Capitolina, Akko, Anthedon, Antipatris & Ascalon* (Jerusalem: Mayer Rosenberger, 1972), 64, no. 218 (Macrinus). See L. Bricault, "Deities from Egypt on Coins of the Southern Levant," *Israel Numismatic Research* 1, (2006): 131, n. 27. A coin of Orthosia (Phoenicia) is known (*BMC Phoenicia*, 126 and plate XVI.1), on which a god (Kronos?) with two lions is depicted.

[36] One very small lead lamella in the Cabinet des Médailles is described by Delatte et Derchain, no. 458 as follows: "un personnage léontocéphale portant le fouet *nḥḥ* et le sceptre *ḥk3* des Égyptiens sur une épaule et appuyé de l'autre main sur un bâton, est debout sur trois lions passant à gauche qui regardent un serpent". Unfortunately nowadays the poor condition of the lead surface does not allow us to see anything on it.

**Figure 4.5**   Bronze coin of Ascalon, from the era of Antoninus Pius, representing Asklepios with three lions.

Reproduced from Internet auction catalogues.

**Figure 4.6**   Bronze coin of Ascalon, from the era of Antoninus Pius, representing Asklepios with three lions.

Reproduced from Internet auction catalogues.

Sometimes his bust over three lions is represented on the coins. Of the six gems:

1. One is kept in Verona, as has been said.
2. Another is kept in Bonn, at the Franz Joseph Dölger Museum[37] (Figure 4.7). The following inscription can be read on its reverse side: ΕΥΤΥΠΙ ΑΣΚΑΗΠΙΟΣ, where it is possible to recognize Εὐτυ<χῆ> Ἀσκ<λ>ηπιός, "good luck, Asklepios!"

---

[37] J. Engemann, s.v. *Glyptik*, *RAC* 11 (1979): 287; E. Zwierlein-Diehl, *Siegel und Abdruck. Antike Gemmen in Bonn. Akademisches Kunstmuseum – Antikesammlung der Universität*, Sonderausstellung 18. Sept. 2002–31. Jan. 2003 (Bonn: Akademisches Kunstmuseum, Antikensammlung der Universität Bonn, 2002), 50–51, no. 114; Ead., *Antike Gemmen und ihr Nachleben* (Berlin: 2007), 219, 459; fig. 783.

**Figure 4.7**  Green jasper stained red kept in the Franz Joseph Dölger Museum, Bonn (drawing from J. Engemann).

Reproduced from s.v. *Glyptik, RAC* 11 (1979): 287.

3. One is in Paris, at the Cabinet des Médailles[38] (Figure 4.8); here Perseus is in front of Poseidon; on the other side, Asklepios is standing on the lions and a monkey is worshipping him.

4. A fourth specimen is kept in the British Museum[39] (Figure 4.9).

5. One has been found in a tomb at Ascalon.[40]

6. Another one was published by S. Ben-Dor.[41]

Moreover, a magnetite stone in the Skoluda collection depicts a standing god wearing an Egyptian crown (two high feathers), accompanied by a lion; the inscription on the reverse side is ΒΑΙΣΟΛΒΑΡ ΧΦΥΡΙ.[42]

Since the time of Hill's publication of Palestinian coins in the British Museum, this god has often been identified as Osiris. Indeed, he is holding the *nekhekh* whip and the *was* sceptre[43] and on his head the *hemhem* crown or the *kalathos* is placed. The *kalathos* is typical of Sarapis, who

---

[38] Delatte, Derchain, no. 423.

[39] Michel, *British*, no. 261.

[40] L.Y. Rahmani, "Copies of Ancient Coins on Jewellery Ancient and Modern," *Israel Numismatic Journal* 5 (1981): 46, plates 11.1–2; Bricault, "Deities from Egypt," 131 and plate 19.19.

[41] S. Ben-Dor, "A Roman Gem from Palestine," *Bull. of the Jewish Palestine Exploration Society* 13 (1947): 171; Rahmani, "Copies," 47, plate 11.3.

[42] S. Michel, *Die magischen Gemmen* (Berlin: 2004), 66, n.339; 283, no. 25.1, plate 26.4.

[43] Osiris is usually holding the *nekhekh* and the *heka* sceptre.

**Figure 4.8A** Brown jasper in the Cabinet des Médailles, Paris, representing Perseus with Poseidon on the obverse, and Asklepios with his lions on the reverse (Delatte, Derchain, no. 423) (photograph by the author).

Reproduced with the permission of the Cabinet des Médailles.

**Figure 4.8B**  Reverse side.

is the Greek and Roman form of Osiris. Hill, in his catalogue of the coins in the British Museum, supposed that the standing god was Osiris and the bust Isis,[44] whereas Meshorer suggested identifying both with Isis,[45] and Bricault with Harpokrates or Horus of Mount Casios.

---

[44] Hill, *BMCPalestine*, lxi–lxii; Rahmani, "Copies," 48.

[45] Meshorer, *City-Coins*, 28; A.R. Bellinger, *The Syrian Tetradrachms of Caracalla and Macrinus*, Numismatic Studies 3 (New York: American Numismatic Society, 1940), 100, n. 165.

**Figure 4.9** Lapis lazuli in the British Museum, London, representing Asklepios Leontouchos.

Reproduced by courtesy of the Trustees of the British Museum.

This god is actually Asklepios Leontouchos, an important god of Ascalon, in honor of whom Proclus wrote a hymn.[46] His Egyptian dress and symbols prove that he is not the god of Epidauros and Cos, but rather a local healing god, similar to the Egyptian Imhotep. The famous architect of the Djoser pyramid at Memphis (Saqqara) was identified as Asklepios, which aroused the belief that he was the true Asklepios.[47] The myth and the cult of Imhotep is very old (there is evidence of it from the XII–XIII dynasties onward) and the Ptolemies contributed to his success. Manetho[48] calls him Imouthes and says that he was a wonderful architect, scribe, and physician, who was therefore identified as Asklepios. He was supposed to be the son of Ptah[49]; hymns to him were written on the wall of Ptah's temple at Karnak, built in the age of Tiberius, and on the gate of Hator's temple at Dendera, built under Claudius.[50] The Egyptian god was connected to Osiris at Phile, in the age of Ptolemy V.[51] When examining the gem in Verona, the observer may consider himself to be regarding the first known image of a god related to Imhotep, that is, the Egyptian Asklepios. Indeed, his similarity to Osiris was perhaps the result of the link between

---

[46] Marinus, *Vita Procli* 19.

[47] *PGM* VII, 629–42. On Imhotep, see D. Wildung, *Imhotep und Amenhotep. Gottwerdung im alten Ägypten*, Münchener Ägyptologische Studien 36 (München: Deutscher Kunstverlag, 1977); and E.M. Ciampini, "Imhotep e i culti iatromantici nell'Egitto faraonico: divinità guaritrici e rigenerazione del cosmo", in *Il culto di Asclepio nell'area mediterranea*, eds. E. De Miro, G. Sfameni Gasparro, and V.Calì, Atti del convegno. Agrigento 20–22 Nov. 2005 (Roma: Gangemi, 2009), 195-200.

[48] *Fragmenta Historicorum Graecorum*, II, ed. K. Müller, Fr. 11.

[49] See the "Daressy stone": Wildung, *Imhotep und Amenhotep*, 25–27.

[50] Wildung, *Imhotep und Amenhotep*; Ciampini, "Imhotep."

[51] Wildung, *Imhotep und Amenhotep*, 157; Ciampini, "Imhotep."

Imhotep and Osiris. The Hellenistic and Roman form of Osiris, that is, Sarapis, was identified with Asklepios at Bethesda.[52]

## DERKETO—ISIS—TYCHE

The goddess at the center of the triad is one of Ascalon's major divinities. A typical goddess of Ascalon was Derketo ("the mighty one"), and her idol was that of a big woman-headed fish.[53] The same goddess is represented on the Seleucid coins of Damascus.[54] Diodorus[55] says that in Ascalon doves were sacred and revered as divinities. Other authors refer to Ascalon's doves[56] as well. In Hierapolis, also in Syria, doves were sacred to Derketo.[57] At Ascalon and Aphrodisias, in Caria, the doves, sacred to Aphrodite, lived undisturbed as it was forbidden to catch them.[58] The dove was also the symbol of Ascalon on late republican and Imperial Age coins.[59] On one coin[60] she wears a moon sickle on her head and is accompanied by a sea Triton.

The Phoenicians, Syrians, and Cypriots often associated doves with Astarte and Aphrodite (identified with Astarte).[61] The bird that the goddess is holding on the gem is a dove. Astarte was another great goddess of Ascalon, often called Palestinian Astarte, or Aphrodite Ourania by her devotees at Delos.[62] A symbol of Astarte's rule over the sea is evident on the coin: the aplustre[63] (the ornament on the ship's stern), and therefore one can deduce that this goddess is also Derketo. Apparently the doves

---

[52] Belayche, *Iudaea-Palaestina*, 463–68.

[53] Diodorus II.4.2–3; cf. Lucianus, *De Dea Syria* 14 (on the goddess of Syrian Hierapolis).

[54] Demetrios III (96–83 B.C.): *Sylloge Numorum Graecorum Copenhague*, no. 420.

[55] Diodorus II.4.6.

[56] Philo, *de Providentia* II.64; cf. Eusebius, *Praeparatio Evangelica* VIII.64); Tibull I.7.17–18.

[57] Lucianus, *De Dea Syria* 14. See P.-L. van Berg, *Corpus Cultus Deae Syriae (CCDS)*. I: *Les sources littéraires* (Leiden: Brill, 1972); E. Will, *Le sanctuaire de la déesse syrienne* (Paris: De Boccard, 1985); J.L. Lightfoot, *Lucian on the Syrian Goddess. Edited with Introduction, Translation, and Commentary* (Oxford: Oxford University Press, 2003); H.-J. Gehrke, "Kulte und Akkulturation. Zur Rolle von religiösen Vorstellungen und Ritualen in kulturellen Austauschprozessen", in *Rom und der Osten im 1. Jahrhundert V. Chr. (Akkulturation oder Kampf der Kulturen?)*. Akten des Humboldt-Kollegs, Verona, 19–21 Februar 2004, eds. H.J. Gehrke and A. Mastrocinque (Cosenza: Lionello Giordano, 2009), 85–144.

[58] Philo, *De providentia*, 2.107 (in Eusebius, *Praeparatio Evangelica* VIII.14); L. Robert, "Les colombes d'Anastase et autres volatiles", *Journal des Savants* (1971): 81–105.

[59] Meshorer, *City-Coins of Eretz Israel*, no. 42; Belayche, *Iudaea-Palaestina*, 227.

[60] Meshorer, *City-Coins of Eretz Israel*, no. 43; see also Fuks, 30.

[61] Lightfoot, *Lucian*, 102.

[62] IDélos 2305; M.F. Baslez, *Recherches sur les conditions de pénétration et de diffusion des religions orientales à Délos (II-I s. avant notre ère)* (Paris: École Normale Supérieure de Jeunes Filles, 1977), 81.

[63] See especially A. Burnett, M. Amandry, and P.P. Ripollès, *Roman Provincial Coinage*, I.1 (London: British Museum Press, 1992), 675–76, n. 4877, 4882, 4885, 4887–4888, 4890.

**Figure 4.10** Bronze coin of Ascalon, from the age of Hadrian, representing the Palestinian Astarte with the crown of Tyche.

Reproduced from Internet auction catalogues.

of Ascalon were sacred to Astarte-Aphrodite also, because the goddess on the gem could possibly represent Aphrodite instead of Derketo.

The presence of the cornucopia indicates that this is the goddess Tyche, who was indeed venerated at Ascalon.[64] The cornucopia was particularly important during the first Hellenistic age, when Seleucos founded Antiochia and created the cultic image of Tyche. Ptolemy I and II both used the cornucopia (or the double cornucopia) as a symbol of their power.[65] The crown decorated with towers and a cornucopia was a common symbol of Tyche and, later, of Fortuna. The goddess on the gem wears a simple crown that is typical of the crown worn by Isis on the gems of Imperial times. On a coin of Ascalon the same goddess also wears the crown of Tyche (Figure 4.10).[66]

During the Hellenistic period many cities chose the most important local female divinity and revered her as the civic Tyche, that is, the protective numen and the personification of the city.[67] The most famous case is that of Kybele at Smyrna, who was represented on the coins as wearing the civic crown. This city-goddess was depicted on a pillar in the basilica at Ascalon (Figure 4.11), of the Severan age.[68] Here the goddess wears a *polos* with an Egyptian ornament, and a small male figure, maybe a priest

[64] Fuks, 30–31; Th. Ganschow, in *LIMC* VIII.1 (Suppl.), s.v. *Askalon*, 535, no. 2.

[65] A. Mastrocinque, "Zeus Kretagenès seleucidico. Da Seleucia a Praeneste (e in Giudea)", *Klio* 84.2 (2002): 355–72.

[66] Rosenberger, *The Rosenberger Israel Collection*, I, no. 165.

[67] See N. Belayche, "Tychè et la Tychè dans les cités de la Palestine romaine", *Syria* 80, (2003): 111–38.

[68] M. Fischer, "The Basilica of Ascalon," in *The Roman and Byzantine Near East: Some Recent Archaeological Research* (*Journal of Roman Archaeology* Suppl. 14) (Ann Arbor: Cushing-Malloy, 1995), 121–48, part. 133–39; Belayche, *Iudaea-Palaestina*, 224.

**Figure 4.11** Pillar in the basilica at Ascalon representing the city-goddess (from the Internet).

of Sarapis, is behind her. The same goddess is representad on the lead weights of Ascalon.[69] One terracotta bust from Ascalon represents Isis–Tyche.[70]

Isis was often seen as the Egyptian form of Aphrodite and the magical gems refer to Aphrodite's images with the name of Isis or vice versa. Moreover, it is easy to explain the presence of the attributes of Isis, Astarte/ Aphrodite, and Tyche in the same divine figure. Modern scholarship has recognized that Ascalon was a Philistine–Phoenician city with strong Egyptian infuences,[71] that is, an intercultural city. Its geographical location is the primary reason for that phenomenon; one hundred years (301–200 BC) of Ptolemaic rule is another.

---

[69] A. Kushnir-Stein, "The City-Goddess on the Weights of Ascalon," *Israel Numismatic Research* 1 (2006): 117–122 (she sometimes holds an aplustre).

[70] D. Flusser, "Gods, Personification and Sea-Monsters," *Sefunim* 3 (1969–71): 22–46, part. 29, plate IV.7.

[71] For example, U. Rappaport, "Gaza and Ascalon in the Persian and Hellenistic Periods in Relation to their Coins," *IEJ* 20 (1970): 75–80; Belayche, *Iudaea-Palaestina*, 224–25; Fuks, 27–28.

# Chapter 5

# EMPOUSA, ALSO CALLED ONOSKELIS

During the Imperial Age, many religious streams claimed that a member of the pantheon, one of the most important gods or goddesses, took a multiplicity of forms. Damascius, the last Neoplatonist, says: "Theologists call the polymorphic gods Aiônes because of the first Aiôn's nature."[1] Indeed, Proteus, for example, is only one feature among a constellation of multiform gods. These divine rulers were continuously changing their forms or contained in themselves all the forms of living beings.

On many magical gems and other monuments an Egyptian god appears (see Figure 3.6, p. 78), whose head is decorated with many animal heads or even with vegetal[2] elements. This god has been known in Egyptian iconography since the first millenium BC. His name varies. In modern literature he is labeled as Pantheos, Bes Pantheos, or a polymorphic god. Sometimes he is depicted with seven or nine heads.[3] The speculations of theologists of the Imperial Age connected this god to the Orphic traditions, as is proved by the inscription on a gem from Byblos.[4] He was considered a creator god, after whom all the living beings in the world were shaped.[5] Several Gnostic sects were interested in the study of this god, who was considered to be the creator and was known by the Egyptians.[6]

A quite ancient Egyptian tradition claimed that the sun god changed his form during the day: He was a lotus leaf in the morning, a lion at noon, and a ram in the evening. Consequently, he could be called Serphouthmouisrô.[7] Several gems and passages of the magical papyri depict four forms of the sun during the day.[8] It was thought by several Gnostic sects that Christ himself was a changeable being, alternately young and old.[9] Like the sun god, the moon goddess was considered to be a changeable being. In particular, the threeform Hekate—who was identified with the

---

[1] Damascius, in Platonis Parmenidem I 50 Westerink, Combès; cf. G. Casadio, "Dall'Aion ellenistico agli eoni-angeli gnostici", *Avallon* 42/2 (1997): 45–62, esp. 54.

[2] J. H. Iliffe, "A Neolithic Celt with Gnostic Inscriptions at Toronto," *AJA* 35 (1931): 304–9.

[3] E. Hornung, *Conceptions of God in Ancient Egypt: The One and the Many* (Ithaca, NY: Cornell University Press, 1982), 127; S. Michel, *Der Pantheos auf magischen Gemmen*, Vorträge aus dem Warburg-Haus, 6 (Berlin: Akademie Verlag, 2002); J.-F. Quack, "The So-called Pantheos. On Polymorphic Deities in Late Egyptian Religion," *Aegyptus et Pannonia* 3 (2006): 175–76.

[4] M. Dunand, *Fouilles de Byblos*, I (Paris: Geuthner, 1939) 44, plate CXXXVII, no. 1248. Cf. R. Janko, "The Derveni Papyrus: An Interim Text," *ZPE* 141(2002): 26; A. Mastrocinque, *Des mystères de Mithra aux mystères de Jésus*, PawB 26 (Stuttgart: Steiner, 2009): 77.

[5] In Egyptian thought: Ph. Derchain, "Le démiurge et la balance", in *Religions en Égypte hellénistique et romaine*. Colloque Strasbourg, 1967 (Paris: Presses Universitaires de France, 1969), 31–34; R. Merkelbach, "Astrologie, Mechanik, Alchimie und Magie im griechsch-römischen Ägypten", *Begegnung von Heidentum und Christentum im spätantiken Ägypten, Riggisberger Berichte* 1, (1993): 57. In the Gnosis: M. Philonenko, "Le 'livre des secrets d'Hénoch'", in *Religions en Égypte hellénistique et romaine*, 109–116.

[6] Hippolytus, *refutatio haeresium* V.7.25.

[7] M.-L. Ryhiner, "A propos des trigrammes panthéists", *Rev. d'Ég.* 29 (1977): 125–36.

[8] A.A. Barb, *Abraxas-Studien*, in *Hommages à W. Deonna*, Collection Latomus 28, (Bruxelles: Latomus, 1957), 67–86; Mastrocinque, *From Jewish Magic*, § 55.

[9] G.G. Stroumsa, "Polymorphie divine et transformations d'un mythologème: l'"Apocryphon de Jean" et ses sources", *Vig Chr* 35 (1981): 412–34.

moon—was called *amoibousa*, "the changing one" or "producing changes."[10]

It is highly probable that the importance given to the polymorphic or metamorphic gods by Imperial Age theologists conferred some dignity on an ancient demon of Greek mythology: Empousa. She was similar to Hekate[11] in that she was a shapeshifter, continuously changing into different animals; she was thought to have one bronze leg[12] in the form of a donkey's leg.[13] She was a popular character of folktales and afterlife scenarios during the age of Aristophanes. As Sarah Iles Johnston[14] has shown, Empousa was the demon who impeded (the name comes apparently from the same root of words such as *empodôn*: "underfoot," or *empodeia*: "impediment") man from going on his way, and especially impeded safe passage of the soul either through the process of initiation[15] or on the way to a safe haven in Hades after death.

This same demon is mentioned in *Solomon's Testament*,[16] a work of the Imperial Age, in which many demons are depicted along with the spells and the angels that could conquer and exorcize them. In this exorcism handbook the demon is called Onoskelis, that is "donkey's leg." It is also evident that he—or she—is none other than Empousa.

As one can see in the lexica, repertories, and encyclopaedias, until now no iconography of Empousa was known. But actually three gems do depict Empousa. One description has been published quite recently. This gem came from Gadara,[17] in Jordan; the other one is larger and clearer in its details (Figure 5.1). It was in the De Clercq collection[18] and is now preserved

[10] See A. Mastrocinque, "The Divinatory Kit from Pergamon and Greek Magic in Late Antiquity," *Journal of Roman Archaeology* 15 (2002): 174–87.

[11] Aristophanes, fr. 515 K.-A.; *Etymologicum Gudianum* 465, 22; cf. Hesychius, s.v. ῎Εμπουσα.

[12] Aristophanes, *Ranae* 288–95.

[13] Scholium in Aristophanis, *Ranæ* 293; *Ecclesiazousæ* 1056. See A. Andrisano, "Empusa, nome parlante (Ar. Ran. 288ss.)?" in *Spoudaiogeloion. Form und Verspottung in der aristophanischen Komoedie*, ed. A. Ercolani (Stuttgart-Weimar: Metzler, 2002), 273–97.

[14] S. Iles Johnston, *Restless Dead. Encounters Between the Living and the Dead in Ancient Greece* (Berkeley: University of California Press, 1999), 133–39.

[15] Iles Johnston, *Restless Dead*, 138, recognizes allusions to initiation rituals in Aristophanes' *Frogs* when Dionysos encounters Empousa in Hades.

[16] 4.1–12 On this treatise see a recent work by S. Iles Johnston, "The Testament of Solomon from Late Antiquity to the Renaissance," in *The Metamorphosis of Magic from Late Antiquity to the Early Modern Period*, eds. J.N. Bremmer, J.R. Veenstra, and B. Wheeler (Leuven: Peeters, 2002), 35–49; here a bibliography can be found. Cf. also a treatise on the properties of stones, attributed to Solomo, I, 8, A. Delatte, ed., "Le traité des plantes planétaires d'un manuscrit de Léningrad", *Annuaire de l'Inst. de Philol. et d'Hist. Orient. et Slaves* 9, 1949 = ΠΑΓΚΑΡΠΕΙΑ. *Mélanges H. Grégoire*, I (Brussels: Secrétariat des Éditions de l'Institut, 1949) 142–77; cf. A. Cosentino, "La tradizione del re Salomone come mago ed esorcista", in *Gemme gnostiche e cultura ellenistica*, ed. A. Mastrocinque, Atti dell'incontro di studio Verona, 22–23 Ottobre 1999, (Bologna: Patron, 2002), 41–59.

[17] M. Henig and M. Whiting, *Engraved Gems from Gadara in Jordan. The Sa'd Collection of Intaglios and Cameos* (Oxford: Oxford University Committee for Archaeology, 1987), no. 424.

[18] A. De Ridder, *Collection De Clercq: Catalogue, T. VII, 2. Les pierres gravées* (Paris: Leroux, 1911), no. 3470.

**Figure 5.1A** Green jasper stained red representing the female demon Onoskelis, in the Cabinet des Médailles, Paris (photograph by the author).

Reproduced with the permission of the Cabinet des Médailles.

**Figure 5.1B** Reverse side.

in the Cabinet des Médailles in Paris. It came from Baghdad. On the obverse side it depicts a demon similar to Hekate, but the demon has one bird's leg and one donkey's leg. Her tail is that of a bird. The same tail is represented on a heliotrope kept in Bonn, on which the goddess has two different legs and feet.[19]

This is not the only case of a goddess or demon derived from Hekate's iconography. For instance, a recipe in the magical papyri[20] orders the cutting of a gem with Hekate's image, but with three heads: one of a horned girl, one of a dog, and a third of a goat. The triple head is reminiscent of the three heads of Cerberus, which were supposed to signify the passing of time, or the forms of the sun.[21] Demons who changed their forms were known to the Neoplatonist Iamblicus.[22] Perhaps these included Empousa or other similar demons.

On the reverse side of the gem depicted in Figure 5.1 in the center one reads: ΦΑΥΣΤΙΝΑ (i.e., Faustina), surrounded by the *palindromon* ΑΒΛΑΝΑΘΑΝΑΛΒΑ (i.e., Ablanathanalba). This magical word can be read in both directions and, when written in a circle, creates a magical ring, keeping everything inside the ring prisoner. In fact a magical papyrus describes a ritual that was able to force someone or something to do what the praticioner wanted by putting him or it at the center of a magical ring.[23] In this case the *palindromon* to be written was

IAEÔBAPHRENEMOUNOTHILARIKRIPHIAEUEAIFIRKIRALITHONUOMENERPHABÔ EAI

Recipes of two magical papyri state that this magical word was equal to the name of the Jewish god[24] and to the snake *ouroboros*, which eats its own tail.[25] This magical gem was typically used for love magic. Faustina was the name of a desired girl and he who used the gem wanted to subdue her and have her at his disposal.[26]

---

[19] E. Zwierlein-Diehl, *Siegel und Abdruck. Antike Gemmen in Bonn. Akademisches Kunstmuseum—Antikesammlung der Universität*, Sonderausstellung 18. Sept. 2002–31. Jan. 2003 (Bonn: Akademisches Kunstmuseum, Antikensammlung der Universität Bonn, 2002), 51, fig. 16, nr. 115.

[20] In *PGM*, IV, 2879–84.

[21] Macrobius I.20.13–17 (the time); Porphyrius, *De signis* 8.52 (the sun); Tzetzes, *Chiliades* II.324 (the time). See R. Pettazzoni, "Il Cerbero" di Serapide", *RA* 31–32 (1948):803–9; S. Aufrère, "Au sujet des représentations du Cerbère de type "macrobien" et pseudo-macrobien: une recherche iconologique", *Res Antiquae* 2 (2005): 3–40.

[22] Iamblicus, *de mysteriis* II.1.

[23] *PGM* V, 304–69.

[24] *PGM* IV, 3069.

[25] *PGM* VII, 579–90; see also Delatte, Derchain, no. 122; *SGG* I, 191. On the Egyptian words in the spell, cf. C. Schmidt, Review of Preisendanz, *Papyri Graecae Magicae*, *GGA* 193 (1931): 443–44; and *GGA* 196 (1934) 177.

[26] With reference to performing magic to obtain love from women, see Chr. A. Faraone, *Ancient Greek Love Magic* (Cambridge, Mass: Harvard University Press, 1999).

# SELECTED BIBLIOGRAPHY

Betz, H.D., ed. *The Greek Magical Papyri in Translation*. Chicago: University of Chicago Press, 1996.

Bonner. C. *Studies in Magical Amulets Chiefly Graeco-Egyptian*. Ann Arbor: University of Michigan Press, 1950.

Daniel, R.W., and F. Maltomini. *Supplementum Magicum*, I–II. Opladen: 1990–1992.

Delatte, A., and Ph. Derchain. *Les intailles magiques gréco-égyptiennes*. Paris: Bibliotheque Nationale, 1964.

Dölger, J.J., ed. *Reallexikon für Antike und Christentum*. Stuttgart: Hiersemann, 1950.

Faraone, Chr. A. *Ancient Greek Love Magic*. Cambridge, Mass: Harvard University Press, 1999.

Kotansky, R. *Greek Magical Amulets*, I, Papyrologica Coloniensia 22. Opladen: Westdeutscher Verlag, 1994.

Lieven, A., von. "Die dritte Reihe der Dekane oder Tradition und Innovation in der spätägyptischen Religion", *ARG* 2, (2000), 32.

Mastrocinque, A. *Studi sul Mitraismo. Il Mitraismo e la magia*. Rome: Giorgio Bretschneider, 1998.

———, ed. *Gemme gnostiche e cultura ellenistica*. Atti dell'incontro di studio Verona 22–23, Oct. 1999, Bologna: Patron, 2002.

———, ed. *Sylloge gemmarum Gnosticarum*, I. Roma: Istituto Poligrafico dello Stato, *Bollettino di Numismatica Monografia*, 2003, 8.2.I.

———. *From Jewish Magic to Gnosticism*, Studien und Texte zu Antike und Christentum 24. Tübingen: Mohr Siebeck, 2005.

———, ed. *Sylloge gemmarum Gnosticarum*, I, Roma: Istituto Poligrafico dello Stato, *Bollettino di Numismatica Monografia*, 2008, 8.2.II.

———. *Des mystères de Mithra aux mystères de Jésus*. PawB 26. Stuttgart: Steiner, 2009.

Merkelbach, R. "Astrologie, Mechanik, Alchimie und Magie im griechschrömischen Ägypten", in *Begegnung von Heidentum und Christentum im spätantiken Ägypten*, Riggisberger Berichte 1 (1993): 49–62.

Michel, S. *Bunte Steine—Dunkle Bilder: Magische Gemmen*. Munich: Biering & Brinkmann, 2001.

———. *Die magischen Gemmen im Britischen Museum*, eds. P. und H. Zazoff. London: British Museum Press, 2001.

———. *Die magischen Gemmen*. Berlin: Akademie Verlag, 2004.

Neugebauer, O., and R.A. Parker. *Egyptian Astronomical Texts 3. Decans, Planets, Constellations and Zodiacs*, 162. London: Lund Humphries, 1960.

Pauly, C., G. Wissowa, and W. Kroll, eds. *Real-Encyclopädie der classischen Altertumswissenschaft*. Stuttgart: Metzler, 1892–1980.

Philipp, H. *Mira et Magica: Gemmen im Ägyptischen Museum der staatlichen Museen*. Mainz: von Zabern, 1986.

Ries, J., and J. M. Sevrin, eds. *Gnosticisme et monde hellénistique, colloque Louvain 1980*. Louvain: Publications de l'Institut Orientaliste de Louvain 27, 1982.

Schwartz, F.M., and J.H. Schwartz. "Engraved Gems in the Collection of the American Numismatic Society I. Ancient Magical Amulets," *ANSMN* 24 (1979):149–97.

Sutherland, C.H.V. et al., eds. *The Roman Imperial Coinage* I–X. London: Spink, 1923–1994.

Université de Strasbourg. Centre de recherches d'histoire des religions. *Religions en Égypte hellénistique et romaine: Colloque de Strasbourg, 16–18 mai, 1967*. Paris: Presses universitare de France, 1969.

Zazoff, P. *Die Antiken Gemmen*. München: Beck, 1983.

Zwierlein-Diehl, E. *Die antiken Gemmen des Kunsthistorischen Museums in Wien*, III. München: Prestel, 1991.

# INDEX

www.ingramcontent.com/pod-product-compliance
Lightning Source LLC
Chambersburg PA
CBHW080928100426
42812CB00007B/2404